Poverty and Conflict in Ireland:
An International Perspective

Poverty and Conflict in Ireland:
An International Perspective

Paddy Hillyard, Bill Rolston
and
Mike Tomlinson

IPA
INSTITUTE OF PUBLIC
ADMINISTRATION

Combat Poverty
Agency *working for a*
poverty-free Ireland

First published 2005
by the
Institute of Public Administration
57–61 Lansdowne Road
Dublin 4

and

Combat Poverty Agency
Bridgewater Centre
Conyngham Road
Islandbridge
Dublin 8

British Library Cataloguing-in-Publication Data
A catalogue record for this book is available from the British Library.

ISBN 1 904541 22 4

This study forms part of the Combat Poverty Agency Research Series, in which it is No. 36.

The views expressed in this text are the authors' own and not necessarily those of Combat Poverty Agency.

Publications and printed matter will be made available, on request, in a range of formats, including audio tape, large print, braille and computer disc.

Cover design by Red Dog Design Consultants, Dublin
Typeset by Computertype Limited, Dublin
Printed in Ireland by Betaprint, Dublin

Table of Contents

List of Figures and Tables

Glossary

ADM	Area Development Management
ASBO	Anti-Social Behaviour Order
CEDAW	Convention on the Elimination of Discrimination Against Women
CFSP	Common Foreign and Security Policy
CHS	Continuous Household Survey
CORI	Conference of Religious of Ireland
CPA	Combat Poverty Agency
CR gas	dibenzoxazepine (used in riot control to make the eyes stream and induce temporary blindness)
CS gas	chlorobenzylidene malonitrile (riot-control gas)
DAC	Development Assistance Committee
DFID	Department for International Development
DPP	District Policing Partnerships
DWP	Department of Work and Pensions (UK)
EAR	European Agency for Reconstruction
ECHO	European Community Humanitarian Aid Office

EEC	European Economic Community
EPIC	Ex-Prisoners Interpretive Centre
ESDP	European Security and Defence Policy
EU	European Union
FES	Family Expenditure Survey
FRS	Family Resources Survey
G8	Organisation representing governments of the eight major industrial democracies
GDP	Gross Domestic Product
GHQ	General Health Questionnaire
HBAI	Households Below Average Income
HIV/AIDS	Human Immunodeficiency Virus/Acquired Immunodeficiency Syndrome
IDPs	Internally Displaced Persons
IFI	International Fund for Ireland
ILO	International Labour Organisation
IMF	International Monetary Fund
INGO	International Non-Governmental Organisation
IRA	Irish Republican Army
KFOR	The Kosovo Force
MDGs	Millennium Development Goals
NAPincl	National Action Plans for Social Inclusion
NAPS	National Anti-Poverty Strategy

NISRA	Northern Ireland Statistical and Research Agency
NTSN	New Targeting Social Need
NUTS	The Nomenclature of Territorial Units for Statistics
OECD	Organisation for Economic Cooperation and Development
OFM/DFM	Office of the First Minister and Deputy First Minister
PSENI	Poverty and Social Exclusion Northern Ireland study
PSNI	Police Service of Northern Ireland
SEUPB	Special EU Programmes Body
SFOR	Nato-led Stabilisation Force for Bosnia and Herzegovina
SPED	Special Purchase of Evacuated Dwelling
TSN	Targeting Social Need
UNDP	United Nations Development Programme
UNHCR	The UN High Commission for Refugees
WEFT	Women Educating for Transformation
WTO	World Trade Organisation

Acknowledgements

Many people have contributed to this report. We are particularly grateful to Margaret Ward who researched the position of women and peace-building. We have drawn heavily on her research and it is hoped that a more extensive treatment of the topic based on her research will be published.

We would like to thank all those who contributed to the special seminars held in Dundalk in November 2003 and who helped shaped the research for this report. In particular, Grace Kelly provided essential support for the seminar itself and provided background research on anti-poverty policies and associated political debates.

Special thanks are due to Agnieszka Martynowicz and Fiona Scullion who helped in a number of ways. Several people read drafts of the report and we were especially grateful to Mick Mann and Liam O'Dowd for comments, advice on sources, and ideas. Our thanks to the anonymous referees in various government departments who commented extensively on an early unpolished draft, which was not intended for outside comment. Paddy Hillyard would like to acknowledge the support of the ESRC in funding 'Reimagining Women's Security in Transition' (Research Grant No. RES-223-25-033), which generated some of the ideas expressed in this report. Finally, we would like to thank all those in Combat Poverty Agency who played a part in seeing what proved to be a difficult project through to fruition. In particular, our thanks to Helen Johnston, Jim Walsh, Tracey O'Brien, Ruth Taillon and Paddy Logue who, from their different perspectives, contributed greatly to the content of the report. We alone, however, remain responsible for the critical analysis and any errors.

Paddy Hillyard
Bill Rolston
Mike Tomlinson   *Belfast, December 2004*

Foreword

Combat Poverty is a state advisory agency developing and promoting evidence-based proposals and measures to combat poverty in Ireland. Our vision is to work for a poverty-free Ireland. Under the Combat Poverty Agency Act 1986, Combat Poverty is tasked to examine the nature, causes and extent of poverty and to advise on policies and programmes to overcome poverty.

Combat Poverty has a specific remit in relation to tackling poverty in the border region through the implementation of a substantial part of the EU-funded Peace II Programme, which it does jointly with Area Development Management Ltd in a partnership known as ADM/CPA. In addition, ADM/CPA is responsible for managing two cross-border measures of the Peace II Programme, along with the Community Foundation for Northern Ireland and Co-operation Ireland. In the context of the Belfast/Good Friday Agreement, the establishment of North/South bodies, and the implementation of the Peace II Programme, Combat Poverty is concerned with the promotion of inclusion, reconciliation and peace-building.

Given the new all-island structures and Combat Poverty's ongoing involvement in the Peace II Programme, Combat Poverty commissioned this research to inform the future development of actions to tackle poverty and promote peace-building in Ireland. The study is intended to promote discussion of the relationships between anti-poverty and social inclusion measures and conflict resolution processes in Ireland, drawing on international experiences. It seeks to throw new light on the two dimensions of the poverty-conflict relationship: poverty as a cause of conflict and poverty as a consequence of conflict, and to inform policies that promote both social inclusion and peace-building.

Policy context

The declared cease-fires of 1994 and the subsequent peace agreement (Belfast/Good Friday Agreement of 1998) provide the context for social inclusion and peace-building in a 'post-conflict' society. The 'Peace Agreement' deals with constitutional and governance arrangements. Economic, social and cultural issues are specifically mentioned but there is little mention of poverty. This is limited to the need for a more focused 'Targeting Social Need' initiative and promoting social inclusion.

The North/South Ministerial Council was established under the Good Friday Agreement. The North/South Ministerial Council brings together those with executive responsibilities in Northern Ireland and Ireland to develop consultation, co-operation and action on an all-island and cross-border basis on matters of mutual interest. Six new North/South implementation bodies were established under the North/South Ministerial Council. The most relevant of these to social inclusion and peace-building is the Special EU Programmes Body (SEUPB).

The SEUPB promotes cross-border co-operation through the administration of the cross-border element of the Peace II Programme and the monitoring and promotion of cross-border activities in the context of the National Development

Plan 2000–2006 for Ireland and the Structural Funds Plans 2000–2006 for Northern Ireland. It is the managing authority for the EU Programme for Peace and Reconciliation in Northern Ireland and the Border Region of Ireland and INTERREG IIIA, and thus has a central role in the promotion of peace-building and social inclusion on an all-island basis.

The Structural Funds Plans North and South each contain a Common Chapter in their respective plans. The Common Chapter sets out a strategic framework for co-operation between Ireland and Northern Ireland. While there is recognition of the economic context, and of the relevant anti-poverty strategies in particular, these are not identified as specific areas for future co-operation and joint approaches. In addressing poverty and conflict, the key collaborative effort has been through the EU-funded Peace Programmes.

The EU funded a Special Support Programme for Peace and Reconciliation in Northern Ireland and the Border Counties of Ireland 1995–1999 (Peace I) and is now funding its successor, the EU Programme for Peace and Reconciliation in Northern Ireland and the Border Region 2000–2004 (Peace II).[1] In Peace I, a Community Initiative Programme, social inclusion and economic development were interlinked with peace and reconciliation, on the basis that disadvantage often feeds and sustains the conflict: it is frequently the most deprived areas that have suffered the most and been the most involved in the conflict. It is axiomatic therefore that socio-economic difficulties must be tackled if the peace process is to be embedded. Thus, Peace I had a focus on targeting actions at the most vulnerable groups and disadvantaged areas.

---

[1]   Peace II has now been extended to 2006.

While the Peace II Programme holds similar objectives, it is set within the Structural Funding criteria as part of a larger funding strategy. This has the advantage of more funding being available, but, as with larger programmes in general, there is less flexibility within the programme. To ensure a peace and reconciliation focus, Peace II contains 'distinctiveness criteria' – funded projects must be either 'addressing the legacy of the conflict' or 'taking opportunities for peace'. Funded projects must also 'pave the way to reconciliation'. Despite the distinctive nature of Peace II, in reality there has been a strong economic focus in the programme at the expense of the social focus. This is highlighted in the Mid-Term Evaluation of the Programme,[2] which has recommended that the social dimension of the Programme be increased.

The other relevant policy context is the anti-poverty strategies in Ireland and Northern Ireland. The revised Irish National Anti-Poverty Strategy *Building an Inclusive Society* was launched in 2002. It made no reference to the impact of the conflict on poverty. This Plan was updated in 2003, as part of the European Social Inclusion process (*National Action Plan against Poverty and Social Exclusion 2003–2005*, NAPincl). NAPincl acknowledges the impact of the conflict: 'The needs of disadvantaged communities are accentuated in the Border regions due to the effects of the conflict in Northern Ireland ... special additional innovative measures are required for the disadvantaged Border regions.' (p. 12)

The recent Annual Report of the Office for Social Inclusion (2004) notes that: 'The border counties of Ireland have been

---

[2] PriceWaterhouseCoopers (2003) *Ex-post Evaluation of Peace I and Mid-Term Evaluation of Peace II*, Special EU Programmes Body.

affected by the Northern Ireland conflict which has contributed to poverty and social exclusion in these areas.'[3] The EU-funded Peace Programme is cited as the main mechanism for supporting these disadvantaged communities.

In Northern Ireland the main anti-poverty strategy has been *Targeting Social Need* (TSN), more recently revised as *New Targeting Social Need* (NTSN). This is one of three spending priorities in Northern Ireland. However, rather than allocating additional resources to areas of social need, the strategy is to 'skew' existing resources towards these areas. The most disadvantaged areas are identified using area-based deprivation indicators and there is a strong focus on redressing 'community differentials', presented as differences between Protestants and Catholics. Northern Ireland is now moving towards an anti-poverty strategy – *Towards an Anti-Poverty Strategy: New TSN – the Way Forward, A Consultation Document*[4] – and has consulted on the approach and content of this broader strategy to tackle poverty and social exclusion.

There is equality and human rights legislation and institutions in both Ireland and Northern Ireland, which also play an important role in addressing poverty and conflict.

---

3   Office for Social Inclusion (2004) *National Action Plan against Poverty and Social Exclusion: Office for Social Inclusion – First Annual Report: Implementation of Plan 2003–2004*, Dublin: Office for Social Inclusion, p. 29.

4   Office of the First Minister and Deputy First Minister (2004) *Towards an Anti-Poverty Strategy: New TSN – the Way Forward, A Consultation Document*, Belfast: Office of First Minister and Deputy First Minister.

Key findings from the research

The review of the international and national literature, and analysis by the authors, identifies a number of key findings. These include:

- Lack of discussion and agreement about the causes and consequences of the conflict in Ireland. As a result it is largely ignored in many policy documents, especially in relation to anti-poverty policy.

- Yet the impact of the conflict has been considerable (3,600 killed and more than 45,000 injured in Northern Ireland). The number of deaths and injuries has been greatest in the most disadvantaged areas. There is a strong, but complex, relationship between poverty and conflict.

- Poverty on its own will not necessarily lead to conflict, but a reduction in poverty and inequalities will reduce the likelihood of conflict. However, when poverty is combined with ethnic, religious or unresolved national divisions, armed conflicts are more likely.

- Societies that are more equal are more stable and more socially cohesive. Levels of inequality may be more important than poverty in relation to levels of violence and conflict. Both poverty and inequality provide contexts where grievances may become politicised.

- Conflicts have a range of economic and social consequences. These include destruction of physical and economic infrastructure, increased expenditure devoted to defence and security, higher mortality and morbidity, mental and physical health problems, a high level of public sector employment and displacement of populations, with associated economic, social and demographic repercussions. A by-product is often an illicit drugs industry. Conflicts in one country often impact on neighbouring countries.

- Experience from other societies that have experienced conflict, such as South Africa, shows that there is a need to focus on social issues, reconciliation and civic participation as well as physical and economic 'reconstruction' in order to build lasting peace and reconciliation.

- The term 'reconstruction' is one of those terms on which there is little common agreement or understanding of what is meant by it. The rebuilding of physical infrastructure and economic regeneration are both important elements of reconstruction but the term has a deeper meaning than that. There is a vital need to reconstruct civil society, education and health services, as well as relationships between communities and individuals.

- Peace agreements are an important framework for reconstruction. The international evidence shows that without peace agreements reconstruction often fails. Peace agreements are typically fragile and only a minority survive more than a decade. In the absence of comprehensive efforts to transcend social divisions, armed conflicts frequently reoccur.

- To rebuild the fabric of society, the following are required:
  - Strengthening good governance;
  - A formal mechanism to address human rights concerns;
  - Disarmament and reintegration of former combatants;

- Building consensus and accountability on law and order;

- Addressing the position of women, children and young people;

- Tackling problems of marginalisation; and

- Strengthening civic participation.

Poverty reduction both contributes to these goals and is dependent on them.

- The involvement of women in peace processes is an essential part of reconstruction. Such an approach also requires a reduction in violent forms of masculinity.

- The report concludes that a full approach to reconstruction has not yet been tried in Ireland. Very little has changed for many people living in the most economically marginalised areas, especially in some inner-city areas in Northern Ireland and in parts of the border counties. The key challenge now is to 'mainstream' peace-building and conflict resolution within anti-poverty strategies and reconstruction programmes.

Policy implications

The authors conclude that anti-poverty policies, in Northern Ireland and Ireland, need to include conflict resolution and conflict prevention. Northern Ireland is currently preparing an anti-poverty strategy. Ireland will be reporting on the progress of its strategy in 2005 and reviewing its strategy in 2006. These contexts provide opportunities to ensure that conflict resolution and peace-building are integral to anti-poverty strategies. Key components should include:

- A recognition of the importance of economic, social and cultural rights underpinning any anti-poverty strategy.

- The need to address income inequalities. This is currently an element of the European Social Inclusion process, but needs to be more explicitly recognised in the *Irish National Action Plan against Poverty and Social Exclusion* (NAPincl), through, for example, a reduction in relative income poverty or the number of people 'at risk of poverty'.

- The need to address other inequalities, as set out in the equality legislation.

- The Irish NAPincl identifies groups at risk of poverty. In the context of poverty reduction and conflict resolution, groups who require particular attention are women, children, young people, victims and ex-combatants.

- Some areas have been more affected by the conflict than others. In Northern Ireland, few areas have escaped being affected by the conflict in some way. In Ireland, the impact has mainly been felt in the border region, although the whole of the country has been touched by the legacy of the conflict.

- The European Social Inclusion process includes the objective of 'Mobilising All Actors'. The evidence from the international research evidence shows that civic participation is crucial in reconstructing post-conflict societies. Efforts must be made to engage all actors in the design and implementation of anti-poverty policy, including those affected by conflict. 'Practice to Policy' work being undertaken by Combat Poverty can play an important role in this regard.

- Co-operation between Northern Ireland and Ireland in the development and implementation of their respective anti-poverty strategies is fundamental in addressing poverty and conflict issues. The responsible authorities – the Office of the First Minister and Deputy First Minister, and the Office for Social Inclusion – are currently working collaboratively on an EU-funded project on Mainstreaming Social Inclusion, led by the Combat Poverty Agency and supported by the National Economic and Social Forum and the European Anti-Poverty Network, as well as partners from France, Portugal, Norway and the Czech Republic. Future work needs to develop and build on this co-operation.

- In the implementation of anti-poverty policies it is important to monitor and evaluate progress on poverty reduction. The EU has devised commonly agreed indicators by which to measure progress on poverty reduction across Europe. Each country is also asked to develop specific national indicators. In the Irish context (North and South) a conflict reduction/peace-building indicator should be developed as part of the work on measuring poverty reduction.

The main reconstruction programmes in Ireland and Northern Ireland to date have been the EU-funded Peace Programmes. Other programmes such as Building Sustainable Prosperity in Northern Ireland and the National Development Plan in Ireland have also had important roles. The EU Community Initiatives, as well as the International Fund for Ireland, have made significant contributions too. This year (2005) discussions are taking place on the future of EU funding. While it is anticipated that the amount of European funding available to

Ireland will be substantially reduced in an enlarged Europe, an important case can be made for funding from the EU and from the Irish and UK Governments to continue the important work of the Peace Programmes. Peace-building and conflict resolution are long-term processes and the progress made to date needs to be built upon in any future 'Peace' Programme.[5]

Any future Peace Programme should include:

- A strong social inclusion focus;
- A conflict reconciliation and peace-building element;
- An economic development dimension;
- Civic participation;
- A transnational element, working with and learning from other post-conflict societies addressing poverty, exclusion and inequality;
- An all-island dimension. While the impact of the conflict is concentrated in Northern Ireland and the Border region, the legacy of the conflict has touched the whole of the island and this should be acknowledged.

Consideration should also be given to the establishment of a North-South Body tasked with tackling poverty, exclusion and inequalities related to the conflict, along the lines of the North-South bodies established under the Belfast/Good Friday Agreement. Such a body would work collaboratively with the relevant Departments in Ireland and Northern Ireland, but would bring an all-island perspective to the work and maximise synergies.

---

[5] See Area Development Management Ltd, Combat Poverty Agency, Co-operation Ireland, Community Foundation for Northern Ireland and Special EU Programmes Body (2003) *Building on Peace: Supporting Peace and Reconciliation after 2006*, Monaghan: ADM/CPA.

Conclusion

This report analyses for the first time in an Irish context the relationships between poverty and conflict. It reviews a comprehensive international literature and applies the lessons to the Irish situation. As expected, the relationship between poverty and conflict is not a straightforward one, but dependent on many contextual factors. Nevertheless, important lessons emerge about how to address poverty and conflict issues in a post-conflict society. These need to be addressed in future anti-poverty policies and reconstruction programmes.

Combat Poverty would like to pay particular tribute to the skill, expertise and patience of the research team, Bill Rolston, Mike Tomlinson, Paddy Hillyard, with Grace Kelly and Margaret Ward. The research team accessed an extensive international literature on the subject, analysed the material and set it within the relevant Irish context.

The work has also provided the opportunity for Combat Poverty to work collaboratively with colleagues in the ADM/CPA Office in Monaghan. This is an important initiative for taking forward joint work on addressing poverty and conflict.

Finally, we hope that this report will inform future work in this area and that the lessons from the work can influence anti-poverty policy and reconstruction programmes as we work towards a peaceful and poverty-free society.

Helen Johnston,
Director of Combat Poverty Agency

The Authors

Paddy Hillyard is Professor of Sociology at Queen's University Belfast where he specialises in research into poverty and inequality.

Bill Rolston is Professor of Sociology at the University of Ulster where the focus of his work is on human rights issues, especially truth commissions.

Mike Tomlinson is Senior Lecturer in Social Policy in the School of Sociology and Social Policy at Queen's University Belfast where he is currently Head of School.

Executive summary

The aim of the study is to explore the international literature on poverty and conflict and draw out the lessons and implications for Ireland. The starting point is the view that armed conflict has had a much greater impact on Irish society than is generally acknowledged. It is argued that there has been a high level of denial surrounding the causes and consequences of armed conflict in Ireland, the most important result of which is to make it difficult to stabilise political institutions and to achieve social reconstruction.

Over 3,600 people have been killed and more than 45,000 people injured. The impact on families and communities has been substantial. An estimated 88,000 households have been affected by the loss of a close relative and 50,000 households contain someone injured in the conflict. Over half the population of Northern Ireland knows someone who has been killed in the conflict.

The international literature shows that the pattern of conflicts since the Second World War has changed significantly. The number of conflicts between states has generally declined, but internal conflicts and civil wars have increased. Casualties of war are now much more likely to be civilians than fighters, and landmines are one of the biggest killers.

Civil wars have a range of economic and social consequences. Most involve massive destruction of the physical infrastructure and communication systems. A large proportion of GDP is devoted to military expenditure in countries with civil wars. Transnational corporations show little accountability or responsibility as they continue trading with one or other or both sides. Contemporary wars cause high mortality and morbidity, and large displacement of populations. They give rise to widespread mental and physical health problems.

Wars within one country have an impact on neighbouring countries. One by-product is a 'war economy', typically dependent on 'conflict commodities' or a flourishing illicit drugs industry. The most common outcome of a civil war is another civil war.

While the relationship between conflict and poverty is complex, nevertheless there is widespread agreement from the research that poverty, underdevelopment, and high levels of inequality are all high risk factors for armed conflict. Both poverty and inequality are implicated as the contexts in which grievances may become politicised. Some 16 of the 20 poorest countries in the world have had a major civil war in the last 15 years. Societies that are more equal are also more socially cohesive than others. Yet all the evidence suggests that income inequality in the world is extreme and growing.

The international research evidence on poverty and conflict points to several major conclusions. Poverty on its own is an insufficient predictor of conflict, and the wealthier the society, the less likely that poverty is a trigger for conflict, especially armed conflict. With developed welfare states and centralised policing, Ireland, North and South, should not be conflict prone. But the international evidence tells us that when poverty is combined with ethnic, religious or unresolved national divisions, armed conflicts are much more likely. Strong states may act to both limit conflict and to perpetuate it. Special geographical and regional factors, often associated with border areas or 'conflict commodities', may provide additional resources and incentives for armed conflict.

A number of different approaches have been taken to reconstruction in post-conflict societies. The World Bank has generally adopted a neo-liberal perspective and has focused on rebuilding the infrastructure and political and economic institutions in the aftermath of violent political conflict. One of the main criticisms made of this narrow approach is that there is no evidence that a focus on economic reconstruction alone necessarily lessens poverty or is sufficient to build peace.

A second approach to reconstruction, as exemplified by many international NGOs, is to focus on rebuilding the fabric of society with a clear commitment to humanitarian ideals. From this perspective, genuine security is not about tanks and guns, but about establishing respect for the rule of law and human rights.

A consistent message from the international experience is that a number of issues need to be addressed. First, there must be some formal mechanism for coming to terms with past human rights abuses. Second, there must be a successful disarmament, demobilisation, repatriation, resettlement and reintegration of former combatants. Third, the specific position of women, children and young people must be addressed. Fourth, civil society must be empowered. Above all, it is essential that the work is *on* conflict rather than *around* or *in* conflict. The success of reconstruction should be measured, not in terms of money or even the standard principles of development, but by whether it contributed to the consolidation of peace and national reconciliation.

In relation to women, the international literature shows clearly that a 'gender-blind' approach to conflict resolution and reconstruction has been a critical element in the global failure to achieve sustainable peace. Gender balance, in terms of the active and equal participation of women in peace processes and in all areas of decision-making, is an essential part of reconstruction. In addition, a sustainable base for future conflict prevention will not be achieved without the examination of discourses around masculinity and steps taken to reduce violent forms of masculinity.

This international literature has direct relevance for poverty and conflict in Ireland. Over the last 30 years the economies of both North and South have undergone profound changes. Market principles and market values now pervade all aspects of life. Both societies have experienced economic growth, particularly in Ireland (South). Unemployment has been markedly reduced. However, there is evidence that both societies are becoming more exclusive and less inclusive. Inequality in income, wealth and health has grown, and significant sections of the population on the island of Ireland live in poverty. Notwithstanding the conflict in the North, the middle classes have done comparatively well compared with the working classes.

The impact of the conflict has been considerable and there is strong evidence to suggest that it has had an adverse effect on the weakest and most deprived sections of the community. The number of deaths and injuries has been greatest in the most disadvantaged areas, and those who have perpetrated a large proportion of the violence have originated from these areas. A new analysis shows the strong relationship between poverty and the conflict. Yet most anti-poverty policies fail to acknowledge the conflict.

The report concludes that there have been a range of lost opportunities in terms of the Irish peace process. Examples abound internationally of valuable and effective progress when key principles have been followed. Reconstruction must not confine itself simply to economic tasks but must prioritise rebuilding society socially and politically. Gender must be at the forefront of reconstruction. Human rights; justice; truth; policing; the needs of ex-combatants, children and young people; and the rebuilding of civil society are central. All of these principles must be at the forefront if peace-building is to be sustained. This is not to say that the programmes have always delivered. However, a detailed audit of the Irish case illustrates the many ways reconstruction has not been tried.

Transcending poverty and conflict in Ireland presents major challenges across all sectors of society. The peace process has failed to establish stable political institutions. In terms of social and economic reconstruction, very little has changed for people living in the most economically marginalised areas, particularly the border region. To some extent, the lack of an economic 'peace dividend' for those communities is offset by the sense that they are moving forward in terms of political representation and gains, but electoral advances as such are no substitute for the exercise of power and the responsibilities that come with government. This is the case for nationalist areas but it does not apply to loyalist areas in the North. The loyalist communities most affected by the conflict have neither seen an economic peace dividend nor an on-going and developing political dividend.

The primary challenge for all sectors is to tackle poverty and social exclusion in the communities most affected by decades of armed conflict. This means 'mainstreaming' peace-building and conflict resolution within anti-poverty strategies and those international programmes ostensibly concerned with reconstruction.

Chapter 1

Exploring Poverty and Conflict

This report sets out to review the international research and experience on poverty and conflict and to explore the lessons for Ireland. The starting point for the study is the lack of attention that has been paid to the links between poverty and conflict, specifically violent conflict as it emerged in Ireland from the 1960s onwards. For the purposes of the study, 'conflict' refers primarily to armed conflict, although in places reference is made to other forms of conflict characteristic of most societies.

While the conflict in Ireland has attracted a vast amount of research, analysis and commentary over the last 35 years, most of this work has concentrated on political issues and debates. Far less attention has been given to the significance of social and economic factors in shaping the conflict. Such factors were part of the early debate surrounding the protests in Northern Ireland for civil and social rights, but they became a side issue once full-scale armed conflict developed in the early 1970s.

From this point on, the political and military crises dominated the agendas of both Irish and British Governments as Northern Ireland exhibited all the characteristics of what would now be called a 'failed state'.[1] In terms of social policy the priority became labour market anti-discrimination policy, and while there was some concern to develop area-based initiatives for the most disadvantaged communities, these were always subordinate to containing the conflict. Nevertheless, economic development was and is a 'crucial area of conflict in Northern Ireland'.[2] Furthermore, social and economic policies and their implementation have 'vital material, symbolic and strategic meanings' which impact on wider political positions and causes.[3] Yet social and economic problems in Ireland (North and South) are not typically linked to conflict in policy discussions. Specifically, the conflict is generally not regarded as relevant to the considerable volume of research and analysis of poverty published in the last ten years.

There is evidence that armed conflict has had a much greater impact on Irish society – and particularly the least well-off communities – than is generally acknowledged. This lack of acknowledgement may seem surprising in the context of the 1998 Agreement and more than ten years of a 'peace process', both of which suggest a willingness to face up to the past and to compromise over the future. Nevertheless, there remains a reluctance to address the direct and indirect consequences of armed conflict in Ireland, partly because there are radically opposing views on who is to blame for the conflict, but also because there has been no decisive victory or defeat. Consequently, it has been very difficult to establish stable all-Ireland and Northern Ireland political institutions and to achieve social reconstruction post-1998.

One of the significant gaps in peace-building has been the lack of systematic research into the links between poverty and conflict. Ireland (South) can rightly claim to be a leader in the development of an anti-poverty policy, but Ireland (North and South) has paid little attention to poverty/conflict linkages. There is a growing international literature on the relationship between poverty and conflict that charts the changing nature of armed conflicts and looks at evidence of the extent to which poverty can be regarded as both a cause and an effect of conflict. Importantly, recent research has been stimulated by a growing recognition within international agencies that neither political interventions nor economic development aid by themselves are sufficient to resolve conflicts and build peace. At the level of policy there is increasing emphasis on ensuring that all forms of intervention are integrated around the objective of conflict reduction and that tackling poverty is an essential part of this.

An immediate problem facing any study of the Irish conflict is the choice of terminology. At the elementary level of language, there is no common set of terms to describe history, the status of the main protagonists or even the territorial entities involved. 'Ireland' can refer to the 'island of Ireland', the '26 counties' or the 'Republic of Ireland', a term that seems to have been eradicated from official representations of 'the South' since 1998. The term 'free state' is still widely used among older generations. There are at least half a dozen terms applied to Northern Ireland: 'the North', the 'north of Ireland', 'Ulster', 'the six counties', 'the province', as well as the officially approved 'Northern Ireland'. This would matter less if there was mutual respect among political opponents for each other's language. But there is not. It is the mark of serious conflict and social division that 'everything is political'.

In this report, we generally use 'Ireland' to denote the whole island and the terms 'North' and 'South' to clarify which side of the border we are discussing. We also use the term 'Northern Ireland'. At a number of points the report discusses the Belfast Agreement otherwise known as the Good Friday Agreement of 1998. For the sake of simplicity, we refer to this as the 1998 Agreement.

One of the questions raised in the course of this research was why social policies, especially anti-poverty policies, are rarely framed in terms of conflict resolution and peace-building. At a specially convened one-day seminar in Dundalk in November 2003, we held a wide-ranging discussion with community activists, voluntary organisation representatives and academics about the peace process and the issue of poverty. It was striking that people working in border areas felt that the peace process had not yielded the expected benefits. The economies of these areas remained restricted and there appeared to be little political momentum behind demilitarisation. Others raised fundamental issues of division and sectarianism, from schooling to residential segregation. Some delegates argued that there was a tendency to ignore the social and economic legacies of the conflict running through many institutions, including the Churches and mass media.

The concept of 'denial' is of value in explaining the lack of attention given to the relationship between poverty and conflict. There is good evidence to support the view that high levels of denial characterise the way the Irish conflict is discussed, past and present, and the way institutions, including governments, deal with the conflict. In his study of 'cultures of denial' the sociologist Stan Cohen argues that we all engage in denial; it is a normal mechanism of survival, protection and equilibrium. It is much more difficult to *acknowledge* violence, injustice, and social separation, and to

4

do something that changes things for the better. But denial is not simply a personal matter, 'it is built into the ideological façade of the state'.[4] At an institutional level, therefore, denial is a crucial mechanism for maintaining the status quo and managing conflict. In some cases, official forms of denial are highly organised; as Cohen argues, they are:

> initiated, structured and sustained by the massive resources of the modern state … In totalitarian societies … the state makes it impossible or dangerous to acknowledge the existence of past and present realities. In more democratic societies, official denial is more subtle – putting a gloss on the truth, setting the public agenda, spin-doctoring, tendentious leaks to the media, selective concern about suitable victims, interpretive denials regarding foreign policy.[5]

Official denial varies not only by type of state regime but also by proximity to violence and injustice. Ireland (South) was very close to the violence in the early years of the conflict and 'taking the war to Dublin' has been an ever-present loyalist threat since the Dublin/Monaghan bombs of 1974.[6] Inevitably, concern about the violence engulfing the whole island has shaped the responses of successive Irish governments to the issue of Northern Ireland.

While arguably more is known about the violence of recent decades than about poverty as such, the social and economic impacts of the conflict have yet to be fully assessed. Put alongside any of the world's current armed conflicts, the amount of death, injury and destruction arising from the Northern Ireland conflict over a 30-year period is relatively minor in absolute terms: it was a 'small war', even if it resonates politically all over the world to wherever generations of Irish people have settled.[7] The legacies and impacts of the conflict resemble to some extent the general pattern of conflicts elsewhere. The difference lies in the specific nature of the conflict and the fact that, unusually, it has occurred in a relatively wealthy part of the world: huge resources have been committed to the control of the conflict.

Estimates of the exact toll of death and injury from the conflict vary: 3,600 deaths and 45,000 injured are typically quoted. In addition, the 'post-war' impact on families and communities is substantial. In the recent study of poverty and social exclusion in Northern Ireland (discussed in detail in Chapter 5) half of all household respondents said they knew someone who had been killed in the conflict.[8] An estimated 88,000 households are affected by the loss of a close relative and 50,000 households contain someone injured in the conflict. Around 28,000 people have been forced to leave work because of intimidation, threats or harassment, and 54,000 households have been forced to move house for similar reasons. These figures only capture those currently living in Northern Ireland; some of the bereaved, injured and intimidated will have moved away. It has been estimated that some 42 per cent of those killed were from the Catholic/nationalist community and 29 per cent from the Protestant/unionist community. About 17 per cent of the conflict-related deaths occurred outside Northern Ireland.[9]

Some commentators argue that the victimisation is much more intense than the bald figures of death and injury might indicate. Using information from the *World Handbook of Political and Social Indicators,* McGarry and O'Leary referred to 'the astonishing scale of the conflict' when seen in a comparative perspective:

Northern Ireland was by far the most internally politically violent of the recognisably continuous liberal democracies during the period 1948–77, both in absolute numbers killed and relatively, as indicated by the per capita death toll.[10]

Another way of expressing this is to calculate the equivalent death toll had the conflict occurred elsewhere. As former Secretary of State for Northern Ireland, John Reid, put it:

[I]f the equivalent number of deaths had occurred in the rest of the United Kingdom, the total recorded number of deaths in Northern Ireland has to be multiplied by 40. That gives a total of between 120,000 and 140,000 people. If the same number of deaths had occurred in the US, it would be equivalent to 480,000 people.[11]

One of the criticisms of police-based statistics of death and injury is that they fail to capture *conflict*-related as opposed to *combat*-related fatalities and ill-health. The shock of witnessing or being closely and personally involved in violent events has directly killed and incapacitated an unknown number of people. Trauma has seriously limited the lives and employment of many.[12] In 1998 the Health and Social Services Inspectorate revealed just how little was known about these effects:

For each person killed or injured there has been an ever-widening circle of individuals affected, socially, psychologically and economically. These include close and extended family members, friends, neighbours, communities, school or work colleagues, church congregations and social contacts ... *The ripples are endless and no-one knows the total number of people affected.* [our emphasis][13]

Our knowledge has not advanced greatly since this was written. We do not know, for example, how many children and young people have had their educational and employment opportunities blighted by the conflict, either by their own direct experience or that of those around them. How has the refugee experience affected people? The conflict has shaped the lives and occupations of many people both within and beyond Northern Ireland. For example, around 350,000 individual members of British armed forces have served in Northern Ireland.[14] Veterans of British armed forces comprised 5.6 per cent of the UK prison population in 2001, though how many had served in Northern Ireland is not known.[15] Tens of thousands of people, mainly men, have been police officers, and thousands more have staffed Northern Ireland's prisons. It is unclear how many people have at one time or another been members of loyalist or republican armed groups, but a quarter of all households in Northern Ireland know someone who has been in prison. Around 80,000 people have spent time in prison as a result of the conflict.[16]

There is little systematic knowledge about the impact of the conflict on individuals and families and the more general legacies of the conflict. In addition, policy responses to the conflict have neglected the link between conflict and poverty in the post-1998 Agreement period. Despite the talk of 'conflict resolution', a number of specific initiatives involving victims, and substantial EU programmes ostensibly designed to build peace, both economic and social development policies remain remarkably silent on the legacies of conflict.

The first objective of this analysis is to review the available international evidence on the relationship between poverty and conflict. Chapter 2 shows that this is both a two-way relationship and a complex one. There is, however, growing recognition that we cannot fully understand poverty without considering conflict and that we cannot simply see armed conflicts as arising from different political aspirations and commitments. Poverty contributes to militarised conflicts, and conflicts contribute to economic underdevelopment and poverty. The most worrying finding is that peace agreements are fragile and only a minority survive more than a decade.[17]

The international literature typically looks at countries and regions characterised by wars whose scale and consequences far exceed those witnessed in the Irish context – at least in absolute terms. Similarly, the extent of poverty in war-torn societies is generally far in excess of the poverty that typifies the group of high-income OECD countries to which Ireland (North and South) belongs.

There are lessons to be learned from the international experience in post-conflict situations. These are explored in Chapter 3, which looks at the concept and practice of reconstruction following armed conflicts. There is a vast amount of experience, good and bad, of how societies move on after armed conflicts. Too often the emphasis is on economic reconstruction to the neglect of other issues. The form that economic reconstruction takes is also important because this shapes the prospects for improving the living standards of those most affected by war.

Reconstruction and peace-building have been heavily criticised as 'gender-blind'. Women are affected by armed conflict in different ways than men and therefore reconstruction needs to address this. As Chapter 3 shows, there is a growing realisation within the international community that without the active participation of women in negotiating peace agreements and in long-term peace-building initiatives, post-conflict social transformation is not effective.

Chapter 4 reviews the evidence on the relationship between poverty and conflict in the Irish context. It begins with an overview of what we know about poverty and moves on to discuss inequality, especially the growth in income inequality. It then focuses specifically on the social impacts of the conflict in as far as these are known and can be measured. New survey evidence that links personal experience of the conflict to material circumstances and well-being is presented in Chapter 5.

In Chapter 6 an assessment of the successes and failures of post-Agreement social and economic reconstruction is presented. Much of this concerns human rights, the reform of policing and criminal justice, demilitarisation and other aspects of conflict resolution, including debates around the potential of a truth commission.

Finally, the report presents conclusions on poverty and conflict. A number of recommendations for mainstreaming the issues of poverty and conflict resolution are proposed. Several of these concern the need for further research on the legacies of the conflict and the need for agreed ways of monitoring progress (or otherwise) on the development of a peaceful and stable society throughout Ireland.

---

[1] This term gained currency following the publication of Michael Ignatieff's book (1998) *The Warrior's Honour: Ethnic Nationalism and the Modern Conscience*, London: Chatto and Windus.

[2] Ruane, J. and Todd, J. (1996) *The Dynamics of Conflict in Northern Ireland: Power, Conflict and Emancipation*, Cambridge: Cambridge University Press, p. 177.

3 Ibid., p. 175.

4 Cohen, S. (2001) *States of Denial: Knowing about atrocities and suffering*, Cambridge: Polity Press, p. 10.

5 Ibid., p.10

6 The bombings occurred on 17 May, which was day three of the Ulster Workers' Council strike that brought down the power-sharing executive established under the Sunningdale Agreement. Notwithstanding the Barron Report (2003), British involvement in these loyalist actions and subsequent threats remains an unresolved issue. See Tomlinson, M., 'Walking backwards into the sunset: British policy and the insecurity of Northern Ireland', in D. Miller (ed.) (1998) *Rethinking Northern Ireland*, London: Longman, pp. 109–110.

7 Tomlinson, M. (1995) 'Can Britain Leave Ireland? The Political Economy of War and Peace', *Race and Class*, 37 (1), 1–22.

8 Hillyard, P. et al. (2003) *Bare Necessities: Poverty and Social Exclusion in Northern Ireland – key findings*, Belfast: Democratic Dialogue, pp. 61–62.

9 Morrissey, M. and Smyth, M. (2002) *Northern Ireland after the Good Friday agreement: victims, grievance, and blame*, London: Pluto Press, p. 65.

10 O'Leary, B. and McGarry, J. (1993) *The Politics of Antagonism: Understanding Northern Ireland*, London: Athlone Press, p. 13.

11 *Hansard*, HC (Session 2001–02), vol. 373, col. 316 (24 October 2001).

12 For example, after the Omagh bombing of 15 August 1998, which killed 29 people, almost 700 people received treatment from the Omagh Community Trauma and Recovery Team. Bolton, D. (2003) 'The Omagh bomb – five years later', *Scope*, July–August. http://www.nicva.org/pdfs/r_SCOPEJulyCover.pdf

13 Northern Ireland Social Services Inspectorate (1998) *Living with the Trauma of the Troubles*, Belfast, p. 4.

14 *Hansard*, HC (Session 2002–03), vol. 411, written answers, col. 374 (20 October 2003).

15 *Hansard*, HC (Session 2003–04), vol. 415, written answers, col. 656 (15 December 2003).

16 Calculated from figures in Hillyard, P. et al. (2003) op. cit. Equivalent figures for Ireland (South) are not available. However, some sense of the extent to which it too has been involved in the war economy is provided by figures such as the following: in 1993 an estimated one-quarter of the state's total law and order budget of IR£940 million was related to the Northern conflict; over the 25 years to that point, an estimated 10.5 per cent of the costs of the war fell on the South, with 7.5 per cent on Britain and 82 per cent on the North. See Tomlinson, M. (1994) *25 Years on: the Costs of War and the Dividends of Peace*, Belfast: West Belfast Economic Forum, pp. 25 and 32.

[17] Brewer, J. (2004) 'Post violence society as a sociological category', Belfast: School of Sociology and Social Policy, Queen's University Belfast.

Chapter 2

Explaining Poverty and Conflict

Research examining the relationship between poverty and conflict has two main starting points. The first asks to what extent poverty causes conflict and, by implication, is concerned with making the case for international action to support economic development and poverty reduction. The second starts with conflict and its resolution but also explores the effects of conflict in generating poverty and underdevelopment. In the last decade or so, there has been increasing interest among researchers, NGOs and the international agencies involved in conflict prevention and post-war economic development, in bringing these two problems of cause and effect together. This is in the wake of widespread disillusionment with the capacity of traditional development policies to improve living standards and reduce conflict.[1] Instead of being associated with rising living standards and international harmony, globalisation is accompanied by political fragmentation, armed conflicts and widespread instability.

The chapter begins by looking at poverty as a cause of conflict. This section includes a discussion of the international concern with poverty and the growth of inequality. The latter, many researchers argue, can be seen as a contributory cause of armed conflict, but the impact of inequality on all forms of conflict also needs to be considered. The next section touches on studies of 'ethno-nationalism' that are broadly unsympathetic to the idea that conflicts should be understood as linked to material factors. We then move on to discuss the changing nature of armed conflict and the challenges this presents to conflict resolution. There are sharp divisions over humanitarian intervention and the degree to which aid, military action, political change and programmes of reconstruction can or should be integrated around a particular international relations policy objective. Armed conflicts require resources and, in turn, structure the economies of zones of conflict. The nature of these 'war economies', their social impacts and regional effects are considered next, followed by a brief section on 'conflict traps' and how in-country and regional armed conflicts have a tendency to reoccur.

Does poverty cause conflict?

There is a growing body of empirical research on the relationship between poverty and conflict. Using a traditional stages model of development, one review, written at the end of the 1960s, showed that there is a 'common insight that the more advanced countries are less subject to political disturbance'.[2] Levels of development that fall short of 'modernity' are more prone to conflict and political unrest, but this is because of the rate of social change associated with modernisation processes. Rapid change may widen the gap between expectations and delivery, and generate uncertainty, an observation that can be applied to specific marginalised groups within highly developed countries.

Three decades later, we find that 16 of the 20 poorest countries in the world have had a major civil war in the last 15 years. In contrast, the high-income OECD countries have few armed conflicts. Ireland is exceptional in this regard. Clearly, armed conflicts are more prevalent in some parts of the world than others. A recent World Bank report showed that Asia, the Middle East and North Africa have had persistently high levels of armed conflicts, notably civil wars.[3] The growth of conflict in Sub-Saharan Africa is such that the incidence of civil war in the region is now on a par with Asia and exceeds that of Latin America. Precisely how the level of economic development might impact on the likelihood of conflict is now of major interest to the research and policy communities.

One recent study looked at data from 152 countries and examined levels of economic activity from 1950 to 1992. In this period the findings were that 'recessions play an important role in determining internal conflict', suggesting that a process of impoverishment rather than modernisation is critical.[4] The probability of an internal conflict breaking out increases between two and three times if a recession is coupled with the presence of an external war. Such findings appear to support the basic assumption behind much development policy that poverty and social exclusion are direct causes of violent conflict. This causal relationship appears to be very loose, however, and the closer a specific conflict is observed, the more complicated the relationship between economic and political factors becomes.

There are many methodological problems involved in establishing statistical relationships between poverty and conflict. As Goodhand argued in 2003, there is limited empirical evidence to support or refute the claim that poverty and social exclusion *cause* violent conflict directly.

Nevertheless, there is widespread agreement in the literature that poverty, underdevelopment, and high levels of inequality, are all high risk factors for armed conflict. In particular, both poverty and inequality are implicated as the contexts in which grievances may become politicised:

> Broadly, it is argued that uneven development processes lead to inequality, exclusion and poverty. This contributes to growing *grievances* particularly when poverty coincides with ethnic, religious, language or regional boundaries. These underlying grievances may explode into open conflict when triggered by external shocks ... or mobilised by conflict entrepreneurs. Although few argue that poverty *per se* causes conflict, research points to the importance of extreme horizontal inequalities as a source of grievance which is used by leaders to mobilise followers and to legitimate violent actions.[5]

There are two further stages in the 'poverty to conflict' process. Firstly, grievances are generated – from historical patterns of development locally and internationally, and from the way the state itself handles social and economic development. Bad governance, particularly state bias towards or against particular groups, provides fuel for the fire:

> A key pattern of escalation is reflected in the process of group identification and mobilisation. Real or perceived economic *and* political differentiation among groups is of fundamental importance to group mobilisation for civil war.[6]

Border areas are especially prone to economic and political marginality, and may act as a 'resource' for rebel organisation and development. Borders can be a resource in other ways, usually by providing revenue streams from smuggling. Once grievances are formed and badly managed, conditions are ripe for violent responses, both 'from below' and 'top down'.

Some researchers argue that another important link in the causal chain is provided by the 'loss of livelihoods', especially for young men.[7] Rebellion has psychological as well as economic functions:

> Violence can offer the opportunity to restore a sense of power and status. It can effect a dramatic and immediate reversal of power relationships, something that may have an immediate attraction to young men ... In a sense the poor have a 'comparative advantage' in violence as they have less to lose. Rebel groups may offer social mobility and a leadership role.[8]

Another important theme is that international efforts to promote development may backfire economically and politically. There is a long history of criticism of models of economic development promoted by a range of international institutions including OECD, WTO, IMF and the World Bank. These include the observation that 'development' often leads to 'underdevelopment', that 'free trade' is typically trade based on terms dictated by the richest countries and that 'aid' is usually tied to the needs and interests of 'donor' countries.[9] The conditions of 'structural adjustment' tied to loans have proved economically destructive and politically destabilising. The specific consequences of international effort are contested, as is the overall impact on global inequality and poverty.

The pattern of recent UN summits is indicative of the international concern with current economic trends and their political impact. All the evidence suggests that income inequality on a world scale is more extreme than at any point

in the twentieth century and is growing. It is estimated that at
the end of the 1990s, the richest fifth of the world's
population possessed 83 per cent of the world's income. The
second richest fifth possessed a further 12 per cent. In
contrast, the poorest two-fifths of the world's population had
a mere 3 per cent. In the 1960s the richest fifth had 30 times
more income than the poorest fifth. They now have 80 times
more income.[10] According to one estimate, the richest 1 per
cent of people in the world receives as much as the bottom
57 per cent put together. It is also argued that as the rich get
richer and the poor poorer, the middle of the income
distribution is disappearing.[11] Recent evidence suggests that
rising average incomes in China and India may now be
reducing the North-South global income gap for individuals,
but the gap between poor and rich countries has worsened.[12]

In the 1990s the UN sought to address the worsening
position through a number of initiatives, including the
Copenhagen Summit (1995) and the Millennium Development
Goals (MDGs) (2000). The latter include the target of halving
the proportion of people who suffer from hunger and who live
on less than one dollar a day, between 1990 and 2015.
Remarkably, the MDGs do not include conflict and/or war
reduction, indicating that the focus on the relationship
between conflict and poverty is a very recent mainstream
concern.

The Report of the Copenhagen Summit records that the
global wealth of countries rose by seven times in the second
half of the twentieth century, yet social marginalisation,
insecurity and violence have intensified. The Summit was
concerned both with the serious levels of 'absolute' poverty
and with 'overall' poverty, the latter term appearing in the Irish
government's national anti-poverty strategy of 1997. The

reduction of inequalities was seen as an important problem alongside the disproportionate burden of poverty, war and environmental degradation carried by women. The report also highlighted the negative impact of excessive military expenditures and the world-wide problem of refugees and internally displaced persons. In framing the challenge of poverty, the Copenhagen Summit linked inequality, military conflict and spending, gender inequality and the displacement of persons.[13]

The Irish and British governments were among the 117 delegations that signed up to the Summit's goals. These included commitments to eradicate absolute poverty, creating an economic, political, social, cultural and legal environment to enable people to achieve social development, and to support full employment as a basic policy goal. The signatories committed themselves to increasing the resources devoted to social development, to achieving gender equality and to promoting social integration based on the enhancement and protection of all human rights.

In the small print of the commitments there were a number of points of direct interest to societies emerging from conflict. The Summit's goals required countries to reinforce peace by promoting tolerance, non-violence and respect for diversity, and by settling disputes by peaceful means. Governance should be inclusive and community development a priority. The signatories are committed to:

> reinforce the means and capacities for people to participate in the formulation and implementation of social and economic policies and programmes through decentralisation, open management of public institutions and strengthening the abilities and opportunities of civil

society and local communities to develop their own organisations, resources and activities.[14]

Other commitments included facilitating the voluntary repatriation of refugees and the safe return and integration of internally displaced persons. Countries were obliged to develop 'as a matter of urgency' policies and strategies to substantially reduce poverty and inequality by target dates. The veterans of wars should be fully integrated into the economy and society.

As indicated, the UN Report addresses both poverty and inequality. It also covers various forms of conflict including military conflict. It reflects some of the sharpest debates within the research community, especially amongst economists, over whether it is 'poverty' or inequality that really matters. More often than not, this is discussed as a moral question of social justice and individual and collective responsibility. But it is also an empirical question about the consequences of growing income inequalities within rich and poor countries.[15] The main arguments revolve around crime, social order, health (especially life expectancy) and domestic violence. On the one hand there are those who do not believe that more inequality is either a bad thing or a cause for concern, providing all incomes are rising. The issue, they argue, is with the very poor and with preventing real incomes from falling. This is challenged by those who point to evidence of increasingly violent social conflict and who appeal to the elementary argument that 'other people's income enters our utility function'.[16] Globalisation has the effect of widening the reference groups we compare ourselves to and broadens the potential basis of political and other conflicts.

So, inequality is implicated not only in armed conflict but also in contributing more generally to social instability. There is a growing body of literature which suggests that the levels of inequality may be more important than the extent of poverty to levels of violence and conflict. From the United States to post-Apartheid South Africa the correlation between inequality and violent crime holds.[17] A study of homicide and robbery over a 30-year period and covering 35 countries found a strong and positive correlation between inequality and crime, going as far as to suggest direct causation from inequality to crime. Although this study was centred on inequality, it also discussed poverty or rather 'poverty alleviation'. One conclusion was that:

> violent crime rates decrease when economic growth improves. Since violent crime is jointly determined by the pattern of income distribution and by the rate of change of national income, we can conclude that faster poverty reduction leads to a decline in national crime rates.[18]

Passion and politics

The 'grievance' link between poverty and conflict is challenged from two angles. There is the argument that most armed conflicts are now the result of ethno-nationalism. In this view, the end of the Cold War unleashed long-standing nationalist forces that produced bloody civil wars in Eastern Europe, the former Soviet Union, and sub-Saharan Africa. Some writers directly challenge economic and materialist explanations of conflict by suggesting that ethno-nationally segmented labour markets and business organisation actually produce political stability rather than antagonism. Furthermore, '[E]conomic theories', writes Horowitz, 'cannot explain the extent of the emotion invested in ethnic conflict ... the passions evoked by ethnic conflict far exceed what might be expected to flow from any fair reckoning of "conflict of interest".'[19] Put simply, blood binds more than any other form of bond. A sense of belonging based on blood is more fundamental and enduring than any other possible bond. The repercussions of such a position for more traditional theories that look at materialist explanations for collective action, including class, are clear.

Referring specifically to civil wars, Fearon and Laitin argue that the key factor is the *resourcing* of conflict:

> the main factors influencing which countries and groups have seen civil war [post-1945] are not cultural differences and ethnic grievances, but rather the conditions that favour insurgency. Insurgency is a technology of military conflict characterised by small, lightly armed bands practising guerrilla warfare from rural base areas. As a form of warfare insurgency can be, and has been, harnessed to diverse political agendas, motivations, and grievances. The concept is most closely associated with communist insurgencies fought in Latin America, Asia, and Africa during the Cold War. But the methods can just as well serve Islamic fundamentalists, ethnic nationalists, or 'rebels' who focus mainly on the production and sale of coca or diamonds.[20]

But these factors are much more applicable to movements based in rural areas, often with remote mountainous terrain.

The other challenge to 'grievance' accounts comes from those who argue that people who engage in violence, whether in organised groups or not, are principally motivated by 'greed'. To sustain armed conflict, rebels need finance, business organisation and good communications. Consistent state policies that prevent rebels developing revenue streams are seen as the main way of curbing armed conflict.[21] In other words, it is not an economic development policy that is needed but expenditure on law enforcement and counter-insurgency to curb arms supplies and flows of money to rebel groups.

The changing nature of conflict

Whatever can be learnt from economic predictors of armed conflicts by way of prevention, the more immediate challenge has always been how to end wars and support post-war reconstruction. But these problems have themselves changed and international institutions designed to deal with conflicts between nation states now find themselves facing very different types of conflict and warfare.

As is widely observed, in the period since the Second World War the pattern of conflicts has changed significantly. The number of conflicts between states has generally declined but internal conflicts and civil wars have increased.[22]

In the early 1950s scarcely 3 per cent of all countries in the world could be characterised as in a state of civil war. By the late 1980s/early 1990s the figure had risen to 17 per cent, subsequently dropping to 12–13 per cent. This is based on a conservative definition of 'civil war' as involving a minimum of '1,000 battle deaths'.[23] Other estimates suggest that up to 27 per cent of countries were involved in civil wars at the beginning of the 1990s, falling back to one-fifth of all countries by the start of the twenty-first century.[24]

The reason for the general upward trend in civil wars has less to do with the number of wars that break out and more to do with their duration. In-country wars last longer than inter-state conflicts because the latter are subject to well-established mechanisms of control. Civil wars do not end at the rate they start – hence the accumulation of conflicts. On average, civil wars last for around seven years and the trend is one of increasing duration.[25] The lack of international intervention, political or otherwise, in the case of many in-country military conflicts may serve to prolong war and is clearly relevant to the Irish case.

The changing nature of armed conflicts is reflected in the consequences for combatants and civilians. Estimates of the impact of wars on civilians tend to be contentious and it is remarkable that there is no single international data set that routinely records the human cost of armed conflicts.[26] Nevertheless, it is generally accepted that the casualties of war are now much more likely to be civilians than fighters. The mass casualties among troops that typified the First World War meant that civilian deaths amounted to about 10 per cent of all deaths from war in the early part of the twentieth century. By the end of the century civilian casualties had risen to 90 per cent.[27] With the 'civilianisation' of war, casualties are now more likely to be women and children rather than men.

A recent UN report (2002) presents graphic evidence of the specific ways women experience war. Violence against women during conflict is described as an 'epidemic':

> We heard accounts of gang rapes, rape camps and mutilation. Of murder and sexual slavery. We saw the scars of brutality so extreme that survival seemed for some a worse fate than death.[28]

Landmines are heavily implicated in the impact of war on civilians. More than a third of all countries in the world are mined and it is estimated that, on average, a mine is triggered every 20 minutes, killing and maiming 26,000 people each year.[29] In 2001 the International Campaign to Ban Landmines reported that 8,000 people had been killed by landmines and about 70 per cent of these were civilian casualties. Two people a day are killed by landmines in Cambodia, 28 per cent of whom are children.[30]

Mercifully, this type of mass-produced weaponry did not feature in Ireland, although the 'home-made' varieties deployed by the IRA against security forces, particularly in border areas, were no less devastating. Civilian casualties – admittedly a contested category – varied according to perpetrator and were around 60 per cent of the overall total.[31] In a recent comparison between Iraq and Northern Ireland, it was observed that in the early phase of conflict the majority of victims were combatants.[32] Civilian casualties rise as the duration of the war lengthens.

Another way in which civilians bear the costs of armed conflicts is through enforced migration – either as refugees crossing international boundaries or as 'internally displaced persons' (IDPs). The UN High Commission for Refugees (UNHCR) provided assistance for 5.3 million IDPs and 12 million refugees in 2001. The impact on some countries is catastrophic. For example, it is estimated that nearly 40 per cent of the population of Afghanistan lives in refugee camps, mainly in Iran and Pakistan.[33] As will be discussed in Chapter 4, there have been refugee and IDP movements in the Irish case, mainly concentrated in the early phase of the conflict.

Conflict resolution

Until the late 1980s, international initiatives to bring civil wars to an end tended to be constrained by the Cold War. For much of this period, the main perspective informing conflict resolution focused on models of practical problem solving of the issues of principal concern to the warring parties. Understanding what is and what isn't negotiable, defining what can and can't be recognised, breaking issues down, confidence-building discussions between influential (but unofficial/non-leadership) actors, all featured as central themes in the theory of 'controlled communication'.[34] The perspective is represented most visibly in the *Journal of Conflict Resolution*, established in 1957. The founders of this journal were committed to collecting and publicising social and political information to provide the empirical basis for predicting war (or peace) in parts of the world that at the time were especially conflict-prone.

Conflict resolution perspectives also involve conflict *prevention* as a goal. This is institutionalised not only in the policy statements of UN and EU conferences but also in specialist units whose function it is to act as early warning systems for impending conflict and/or social crisis. Indeed much of the institution building within the EU is now around themes of international peace and security.

With the break-up of Yugoslavia, 'peace-keeping' as well as 'humanitarian intervention' became more common. In 1992 the EU established the European Community Humanitarian Aid Office (ECHO).[35] In less than a decade, the autonomy of ECHO is under threat as the EU has moved from being a purely civilian organisation to one that seeks to integrate defence, foreign policy and other concerns.[36] As a recent statement on 'security strategy' put it:

26

The point of the Common Foreign and Security Policy
and European Security and Defence Policy is that we
are stronger when we act together ... The challenge now
is to bring together the different instruments and
capabilities: European assistance programmes and
the European Development Fund, military and civilian
capabilities from Member States and other instruments.
All of these can have an impact on our security and
on that of third countries. Security is the first condition
for development. Diplomatic efforts, development,
trade and environmental policies should follow the
same agenda. In a crisis there is no substitute for unity
of command.[37]

The Common Foreign and Security Policy (CFSP) and
European Security and Defence Policy (ESDP) now seek to
incorporate humanitarian aid within foreign policy concerns,
including the fight against terrorism. The formation of the
Rapid Reaction Force is designed to strengthen the EU's
role in the 'Petersberg tasks', which include humanitarian
and rescue tasks, peace-keeping, crisis management and
peace-making. Unlike the Balkans, the Irish conflict has not
presented a serious threat to European security, although the
development of EU defence and foreign policies in the 1990s
coincides with the Irish peace process and EU Peace
programmes.

Inevitably, such developments have been accompanied by
sharp debates within the conflict resolution literature over the
role of third party and international interventions. There are
issues of the timing of such interventions as well as the level
at which influence is brought to bear. The dilemma of
reinforcing existing power relations and institutional
arrangements, as opposed to supporting political change,

remains a key problem. One issue concerns how reconstruction funds should be channelled. Using established governmental agencies and policies to disburse international peace-building funds may undermine the objectives of international intervention and divert funds away from the social and economic development in areas most affected by conflict.[38]

International involvement is never interest-free but there are important differences between approaches based on coercive 'sticks and carrots' packages and those based on an ethos of non-coercive, 'win-win' problem solving.[39] In particular, there is a polarisation between those pushing to integrate military, political and humanitarian crisis intervention and those seeking to defend traditions of impartiality.[40] These 'old rules' provided guidance to those supplying humanitarian aid and protection as to how they should relate to conflicting parties and aid donors. Neutrality and impartiality were key principles:

> non-combatants are entitled to assistance and protection in proportion to their need, and not according to their political affiliation, religion, race or creed. More practically, humanitarian access has been contingent upon the principle of neutrality: not taking a position with regard to the justness of any particular cause. Importantly, these principles implied a separation of what might be called 'humanitarian politics' from the partisan politics of the warring parties and interventions or interests of other states. In donor organisations, this separation was marked by institutional and funding arrangements that underscored the independent and unconditional character of emergency assistance.[41]

The 'new humanitarianism' uses aid and development as tools of political leverage, at best contributing to the reduction of conflict, at worst providing excuses for war and occupation. In such politicised contexts, NGOs and international agencies – including the International Red Cross – have become military targets. This has led to an increasingly intense debate within the NGO and International NGO (INGO) community over the issue of 'conditionality', tying aid to demands for democratisation, human rights, etc. Humanitarian maximalists link humanitarian assistance to development and peace-building and argue that this is evidence of a 'joined up' strategy. They are frequently criticised by minimalists for distorting humanitarian principles by using aid for political rather than humanitarian purposes. Humanitarian minimalists on the other hand define aid as simply saving lives. They argue that it is time to 'go back to basics' and focus on the efficiency of aid delivery and distribution.[42]

In the last decade two further criticisms of conflict resolution have come to the fore. The first is critical of conflict 'resolution' as the mere absence of war. Conflict resolution may be defined as 'the process of resolving a dispute or a conflict permanently, by providing each side's needs, and adequately addressing their interests so that they are satisfied with the outcome'.[43] As such, it is an improvement on the concept of 'conflict management' which implies that 'the goal is the reduction or control of volatility more than dealing with the real source of the problem.'[44] At the same time, many theorists now argue that what is necessary is a focus on the notion of 'conflict transformation', which implies taking seriously the structural bases of conflict and tackling those structures rather than merely attempting to change attitudes. Such an approach must involve, as Lederach argues, 'the identification and acknowledgment of what happened (i.e. truth), an effort to right the wrongs that occurred (i.e. justice) and forgiveness for the perpetrators (mercy).'[45]

A top-down political negotiation or intervention leading to a deal of some sort does little of itself to address the interests, concerns and involvement of local communities for which conflict or war has been an historical reality. Successful conflict resolution, it is argued, needs to involve transformation of the social and economic circumstances of communities caught up in, or mobilised around, conflict.[46] In this view, community development is essential to peace-building, which has to be constructed 'from below' and on the basis of addressing global underdevelopment in a manner that genuinely challenges inequality and exclusion.

The second criticism of mainstream conflict resolution is that it is patriarchal in nature. It is patriarchal if it fails to address the specific ways in which women experience war and peace-building. Women and girls are prime targets in armed conflicts because they are seen as the bearers of cultural identity. Gender-based sexual violence has become a weapon of war, as illustrated earlier. Women are also actively involved in war – for instance as combatants, as ancillary workers for military groups, and as providers of a whole range of communal supports for social movements.[47] Conflict resolution is patriarchal if there is no attempt to incorporate women in peace-building processes and to transform the cultures of male domination and violence that underpin and reproduce war.[48]

War economies

Conflict resolution involves more than political negotiation, humanitarian intervention and dealing with the immediate aftermath of war. Armed conflicts, particularly long-term ones, establish a distinctive type of economy, which usually includes a substantial deterioration in living standards.

The economic impact of civil wars was recently surveyed in a major World Bank policy report on civil war and development policy.[49] The report begins by demonstrating that civil war is 'development in reverse'. The first and most obvious economic loss from civil war arises from the destruction of property, physical infrastructure such as roads and bridges, energy supplies and telecommunications. All forms of private and public capital goods – from buses and schools to bicycles and cattle – come under threat of destruction or appropriation.

Another consequence of war is capital flight. Mobile private wealth is rapidly shifted to safer investments in safer places. Businesses that remain are undermined by uncertainty, shortened time horizons and criminal opportunism. Civil war economies often develop substantial 'shadow economies' as formal systems of taxation and distribution are undermined.

A third feature of civil war countries is the proportion of GDP devoted to military expenditure, rising on average to 5 per cent. The World Bank report shows that, when wars end, military spending rarely returns to pre-war levels:

> The government often presents the modest reduction in military spending from its wartime level as a peace dividend, but a more accurate way of viewing post-conflict military spending is to see it as a major hidden

cost of conflict, hidden because abnormally inflated military spending persists long after the conflict is over.[50]

As might be expected, the overall economic effect of civil wars is to slow the rate of growth (on average by 2.2 percentage points),[51] often resulting in negative growth rates, a decline in personal incomes, and increases in absolute and relative poverty levels. For example, a study of the Basque country argued that up until ETA's cease-fire in 1998, there had been a conflict-related 10 per cent fall in per capita GDP since 1975.[52]

This is not to suggest that everyone loses from civil war. The international arms trade is the most obvious beneficiary and the most obvious candidate for regulation and curtailment. Wars need to be financed and both sides may come to rely on the exploitation and control of so-called 'conflict commodities' such as oil, diamonds or timber, even to the extent of preventing negotiations between parties.[53] Transnational corporations continue to trade with civil war countries, leading to calls from many NGOs for greater corporate accountability and responsibility.

Most of the above points apply to Ireland. The conflict is characterised by high levels of military spending. The armed groups may not have any 'conflict commodities' to rely on but they do have an economic base. Physical destruction has been substantial and extends well beyond the confines of Northern Ireland. In Chapter 4 the economic impacts of the conflict are looked at more closely.

Social costs

As mentioned earlier, the direct human costs of civil war are principally fatalities and population displacement. One observation is that civil war increases adult and infant mortality, sometimes dramatically, as in the case of Liberia and Afghanistan. It is difficult to generalise on the direct cause of these inflated mortality rates. In addition to the deaths caused by combat, high mortality rates caused by infectious diseases are characteristic of refugee camps and among IDP settlements.

High mortality and morbidity rates persist after civil wars. One study attributes this to a combination of 'technical regress' and 'budget reduction'. The former refers to the impact of war in worsening the conditions for maintaining good health, conditions that may remain for many years. Civil war also reduces the spending available for health care, which is constrained in the post-conflict period by continuing high levels of military expenditure.[54]

The reduction in health-care infrastructure, combined with high rates of infection among soldiers, means that HIV/AIDS and other sexually transmitted diseases spread at a faster rate. There is evidence from Rwanda, Sierra Leone, Liberia and Mozambique that the spread of HIV/AIDS through rape was deliberate and systematic.[55]

The above observations are not typical of the Irish experience. On the other hand, there is evidence of considerable effects on mental health (see Chapter 4). Psychological damage experienced by combatants and civilians is often neglected in discussions of the impact of war. Mental health is less well-researched than physical health and it is also more contentious. There is recent evidence from Bosnia,[56] Sierra Leone[57] and Sri Lanka[58] of deep and long-lasting trauma and depression, resulting in the transmission of trauma between generations and elevated suicide rates. Some commentators challenge the universal application of western individualistic models of 'trauma' and psychological damage. Using Bosnia, Rwanda and Nicaragua as his main examples, Summerfield presents a critique of psychosocial projects that draw on western trauma models. He argues that a key aspect of contemporary political violence is to terrorise 'the entire fabric of grassroots social relations, as well as subjective mental life as a means of social control'.[59] He argues that for survivor populations to manage their suffering and to adapt and recover, they need a collective focus:

> Emphasis should be placed on social development/ rehabilitation principles, to which can be grafted those additional issues thrown up by crises which are man-made rather than natural. In particular, this means an overall approach which locates the quest of victims for rights and justice as a central and not peripheral issue.[60]

Whatever model is adopted, there is evidence of major effects on mental health in relation to the conflict in Ireland, as we will discuss in Chapter 4.

Regional effects

Wars within a country can frequently be caused or exacerbated by processes in neighbouring countries. A key example of this is the conflict in the Democratic Republic of the Congo, linked as it is to more general conflict in the Great Lakes region.[61]

Likewise, the costs of war are rarely felt solely in one country, even with civil war as the dominant form of armed conflict.

Parties to conflicts have political and economic relationships with actors and states elsewhere and may be part of powerful trading or political networks. This is clearly an important issue in the case of Ireland. The nature of these links will be such as to draw neighbouring territories into conflicts to a lesser or greater extent and some of the consequences may lie much further afield. It has even been claimed that 'many of the costs of civil war, indeed, probably most of them, accrue outside the affected country'.[62]

Some of the reasons for this are already clear. Armed conflicts generate large numbers of refugees and the safest place to be is very probably outside of the country or disputed territory. Between 1975 and 1995, the global total number of refugees rose from 2 to 15 million people.[63] In 2002 there were 20.6 million persons 'of concern' to UNHCR throughout the world, only 2 million of whom were in EU countries. Although relatively speaking this number is small and easily accommodated – Pakistan alone houses this many refugees from Afghanistan – there are concerted efforts to keep refugees out of Europe altogether. With racism against asylum seekers and refugees reaching new heights, policy proposals for global networks of camps outside the EU to 'process' those fleeing persecution and war are becoming more common.[64] Both Britain and Ireland are embroiled in the politics of refugees and asylum seekers, in addition to the much less talked about conflict-related movement of people out of Northern Ireland, either across the border, to Britain or elsewhere.

One of the by-products of certain countries with armed conflicts is a flourishing illicit drugs industry: 'civil war creates territory outside the control of a recognised government on which drugs can be cultivated'.[65] But the effects of that industry are felt most acutely in the richest countries, where per capita consumption of heroin and cocaine is highest. Three-quarters of coca production takes place in Colombia, while an estimated 70 per cent of opium comes from Afghanistan. Heroin trafficking routes to Europe have exploited conflict or post-conflict conditions, either using the 'traditional' route through Pakistan, Iran, Turkey and the Balkans, or the northern 'silk road' through Tajikistan and the Russian Federation.[66]

The conflicts that facilitate the illegal hard drugs industry are related, therefore, to the death, morbidity and violence associated with heroin and cocaine consumption in the richest markets of the USA, Europe and Australia. These regions spend vast resources on criminalising drug use to the point where the majority of prison populations are made up of drug-related offenders. The drugs trade may also become a major resource for armed groups, as it seems to have become for some of the loyalist groups in Northern Ireland.[67]

As well as these global connections, countries in conflict have distinct effects on neighbouring countries. High military expenditure in conflict countries encourages higher military spending among neighbours, 'partly because of norm setting and the emulation and rivalries of military leaderships'.[68] Neighbouring territories may become involved in controlling the regional spillover effects of civil wars, seeking to minimise regional non-investment and capital flight.

Conflict traps

The latest research on poverty and civil wars makes gloomy reading regarding the prospects for peace. Armed conflicts intensify hatreds, and interests become more and more organised around the conflict.

In the early years of civil wars the probability of 'peace' (that is, a cessation of armed conflict) appears to deteriorate quite sharply. It then improves gradually, but wars are particularly lengthy in societies composed of two or three distinct groups, probably because 'this makes creating distinct identities of support easier for both rebels and government'.[69] In some instances the social polarisation is directly reflected in patterns of poverty and inequality.[70] There are clear parallels with Ireland here.

The most common outcome of a civil war is another civil war. Countries that have had a war are up to four times more likely to experience another war and this is likely to occur within a decade. Only 21 of the 110 armed conflicts between 1989 and 1999 ended with peace agreements (rather than a victory by one side or the partitioning of territory) and very few of these survived.[71] It may take up to 30 years before peace is properly embedded. The lesson of conflicts all over the world is that unless specific measures are taken to institutionalise peace, conflicts break out again sooner or later.

Conclusion

It is relatively uncomplicated to describe how conflict affects economic activity and causes poverty, and there is general agreement that 'protracted conflicts are likely to produce chronic poverty'.[72] But even with this generalisation it is important to distinguish specific ways in which violence shapes the economy. War-related sectors may grow; at the same time the conflict may involve economic targets and blockades, in addition to stimulating the development of 'shadow' economic activity, lawlessness and insecurity. Border areas are particularly implicated as 'incubators' of conflict and poverty, though as we have argued in the case of Ireland, this is not necessarily the dominant factor.

Both 'greed' and 'grievance' play a role in generating and sustaining conflict and poverty. If poverty and underdevelopment are seen as the primary causes of conflict, then aid and development policies will probably fail because they ignore politics and governance. This view is reflected in the conclusions of the World Bank report on civil war and development policy:

> Peace is not officially included as a Millennium Development Goal, yet at a minimum it is important as an instrument for attaining these goals ... peace can be seen as a core objective of the international community ... [which] could adopt the same approach to reducing the incidence of civil war as it has to the objective of reducing world poverty. It could set a target, such as halving the incidence of civil war by 2015.[73]

Peace-building involves strengthening good governance, addressing human rights concerns, tackling problems of political marginalisation, building consensus and accountability around law and order, and strengthening civic participation.[74] Inequality and poverty reduction both contribute to such goals and are dependent on them. In the next chapter we explore this issue of how reconstruction is carried out after military conflicts.

---

[1] See for example Stiglitz, J. (2002) *Globalisation and its discontents*, New York: Norton, W. W. and Co.

2   Feierabend, I. K., Feierabend, R. L. and Nesvold. B. N. (1969) 'Social change and political violence: Cross-national patterns', in H. D. Graham and T. R. Gurr (eds.) *Violence in America*, New York: Bantam, pp. 632–687.

3   Collier, P. et al. (2003) *Breaking the Conflict Trap: Civil War and Development Policy*, Oxford: Oxford University Press/World Bank.

4   Blomberg, S. and Hess, G. (2002) 'The Temporal Links between Conflict and Economic Activity', *Journal of Conflict Resolution,* 46 (1), 89.

5   Goodhand, J. (2003) 'Enduring Disorder and Persistent Poverty: a review of the linkages between war and chronic poverty', *World Development*, 31 (3), 635.

6   Verstegen, S. (2001) *Poverty and Conflict: an entitlement perspective*, Brussels: Conflict Prevention Network, p. 15.

7   Ohlsson, L. (2000) *Livelihood Conflicts: Linking poverty and environment as causes of conflict*, Stockholm: SIDA.

8   Goodhand, J. (2003) op. cit., p. 637.

9   See for example George, S. (1992) *The debt boomerang: how third world debt harms us all*, London: Pluto Press; Hayter, T. and Watson, C. (1985) *Aid: rhetoric and reality*, London: Pluto Press; Frank, A. G. (1978) *Dependent accumulation and underdevelopment*, London: Macmillan.

10 World Bank (2000) *World Development Report 2000/2001*. http://econ.worldbank.org/wdr/poverty

11 Milanovic, B. (2002) 'True World Income Distribution, 1988 and 1993: First Calculations Based on Household Surveys Alone', *Economic Journal*, 112, January, pp. 51–92.

12 Milanovic, B. (2004) 'Half a World: Regional inequality in five great federations', World Bank. http://econwpa.wustl.edu:80/eps/urb/papers/0404/0404002.pdf

13 United Nations (1995) *Report of the World Summit for Social Development (Copenhagen 6–12 March)*, New York: United Nations.

14 Ibid., Commitment 1 (c), p. 8.

15 Jencks, C. (2002) 'Does Inequality Matter?' *Daedalus,* winter, 49–65.

16 Milanovic, B. (2003) 'Why we all do care about inequality (but are loath to admit it)', World Bank. http://ssrn.com/abstract=530363

17 For the United States see Kelly, M. (2000) 'Inequality and Crime', *The Review of Economics and Statistics,* 82 (4), 530–539. See also Demombynes, G. and Özler, B. (2002) *Crime and Local Inequality in South Africa*, World Bank Policy Research Working Paper 2925; and Hsieh, C. and Pugh, M.D. (1993) 'Poverty, Inequality, and Violent Crime: A Meta-Analysis of Recent Aggregate Data Studies', *Criminal Justice Review,* 18 (2), 182–202.

18 Fajnzylber, P., Lederman, D. and Loayza, N. (2002) 'Inequality and Violent Crime', *The Journal of Law and Economics*, 45, 1–39.

19 Horowitz, D. L. (2000) *Ethnic Groups in Conflict,* Los Angeles: University of California Press (2nd edn.), pp. 134–135. See also Connor, W. (1994) *Ethnonationalism: The Quest for Understanding*, Princeton: Princeton University Press.

20 Fearon, J. and Laitin, D. (2003) 'Ethnicity, Insurgency and Civil War', *American Political Science Review,* 97 (1), 75–90.

21 Collier, P. et al. (2003) op. cit., pp. 125–132.

22 Duffield, M. (2000) 'Globalisation, transborder trade and war economies', in M. Berdal and D. Malone (eds.) *Greed and Grievance. Economic agendas in civil wars*, Boulder, Colorado: Lynne Reiner, pp. 69–90.

23 Gleditsch, N. et al. (2002) 'Armed Conflict 1946–2001: A New Dataset', *Journal of Peace Research*, 39 (5), 616–637.

24 Fearon, J. and Laitin, D. (2003) op. cit.

25 Collier, P., Hoeffler, A. and Söderbom M. (2001) *On the Duration of Civil War*, World Bank Policy Research Working Paper 2681, Washington D.C.

26 Mack, A. (2002) 'Civil War: Academic Research and the Policy Community', *Journal of Peace Research*, 39 (5), 515–525.

27 Cairns, E. (1997) *A Safer Future: Reducing the Human Cost of War*, Oxford: Oxfam Publications.

28 Rehn, E. and Sirleaf, E. J. (2002) *Women, War, Peace: The Independent Experts' Assessment*, UNIFEM, p. 9. http://www.unifem.org/

29 Vietnam Veterans Association of America, *Annual Report for 1999*, Washington.

30 International Campaign to Ban Landmines (2002) *Landmine Monitor Report 2002: Toward a Mine Free World*, New York: Human Rights Watch. http://www.icbl.org

31 This figure applies to the period 1969–1993. See 'Northern Ireland: the Facts', *New Internationalist*, 255, May 1994. http://www.newint.org/

32 Hewitt, C. (2003) 'Outside View: Iraq and Northern Ireland', *Washington Times,* 17 November.

33 Collier, P. et al. (2003) op cit.

34 Burton, J. (1987) *Resolving deep-rooted conflict: A handbook*, Lanham: University Press of America.

35 See http://europa.eu.int/comm/echo

36 See Statewatch, 'Global Policing Role for EU'. http://www.statewatch.org/news/dec00/nonmil.htm

37 *A Secure Europe in a Better World*, European Security Strategy, Brussels, 12 December 2003, p. 13.

38 Burton, J. (1987) op. cit.

39 Curle, A. (1971) *Making Peace*, London: Tavistock; Kelman, H. (1972) 'The problem-solving workshop in conflict resolution', in R. Merritt, *Communication in International Politics*, Illinois: University of Illinois Press, pp. 168–204; Burton, J. (ed.) (1990) *Conflict: Human needs theory*, London: Macmillan.

40 Duffield, M. (2001) *Global Governance and the new Wars, The merging of security and development*, London: Zed Books.

41 Macrae, J., Brusset, E. and Tiberghien, E. (2003) 'Coherence or cooption? Europe and the new humanitarianism', in *Europe in the World: Essays on EU foreign, security and development policies*, London: Bond, pp. 9–17.

42 Goodhand, J. with Atkinson, P. (2001) *Conflict and Aid: Enhancing the Peacebuilding Impact of International Engagement. A Synthesis of Findings from Afghanistan, Liberia and Sri Lanka*. London: International Alert.

43 International Online Training Program on Intractable Conflict, Conflict Research Consortium, University of Colorado. http://www.colorado.edu/conflict/peace/

44 Ibid.

45 Quoted in ibid.

46 Miall, H. et al. (1999) *Contemporary conflict resolution. The prevention, management and transformation of deadly conflicts*, Cambridge: Polity Press.

47 United Nations Security Council (2002) *Report of the Secretary General on Women, Peace and Security*, United Nations Publications.

48 Pankhurst, D. (2000) *Women, Gender and Peacebuilding*, University of Bradford, Centre for Conflict Resolution, Working Paper No. 5.

49 Collier, P. et al. (2003) op. cit.

50 Ibid., pp. 20–21.

51 Ibid., p. 17.

52 Abadie, A. and Gardeazabal, J. (2001) *The Economic Costs of Conflict: A Case-Control Study for the Basque Country*, Massachusetts: National Bureau of Economic Research, Working Paper No. 8478.

53 Pauwels, N. (2004) 'War economies: EU Options', in H. Mollett (ed.) *Europe in the World: Essays on EU foreign, security and development policies*, London: Bond.

54 Ghobarah, H., Huth, P. and Russett, B. (2003) 'Civil Wars Kill and Maim People – Long After the Shooting Stops'. http://www.cbrss.harvard.edu/programs/hsecurity/papers/june/ghobara h.pdf

55 Collier, P. et al. (2003) op. cit., p. 28.

56 Mollica, R. F. et al. (2001) 'Longitudinal Study of Psychiatric Symptoms, Disability, Mortality and Emigration among Bosnian Refugees', *Journal of the American Medical Association*, 286 (5), 546–554.

57 Collier, P. et al. (2003) op. cit., p. 28.

58 Somasundaram, D. (1998) *Scarred Minds: The Psychological Impact of War on Sri Lankan Tamils*, New Delhi: Vedams. See also Collier, P. et al. (2003) op. cit., pp. 29–30.

59 Summerfield, D. (1996) *The impact of war and atrocity on civilian populations: Basic Principles for NGO Interventions and a Critique of Psychosocial Trauma Projects*, London: Relief and Rehabilitation Network, p. 4.

60 Ibid., p. 3.

61 Del Castillo, G. (2003) *Economic Reconstruction in Post-Conflict Transitions: Lessons for the Democratic Republic of the Congo (DRC)*, Paris: OECD Development Centre. http://www.oecd.org/dev/technics

62 Collier, P. et al. (2003) op. cit., p. 48.

63 UNHCR (2003). http://www.unhcr.ch

64 See for example Britain's 'new vision for refugees' discussed in Hayes, B. and Bunyan, T., 'Migration, Development and the EU Security Agenda', in H. Mollett (ed.) *Europe in the World: Essays on EU foreign, security and development policies*, London: Bond.

65 Collier, P. et al. (2003) op. cit., p. 44.

66 United Nations Office on Drugs and Crime (2003) *Global Illicit Drug Trends 2003*, New York: United Nations.

67 Organised Crime Task Force (2004) *Confronting the Threat: serious and organised crime in Northern Ireland. Threat Assessment and Strategy*, Belfast: Northern Ireland Office.

68 Collier, P. et al. (2003) op. cit., p. 34.

69 Ibid., p. 81.

70 See for example Bisogno, M. and Chong, A. (2002) 'Poverty and Inequality in Bosnia and Herzegovina after the civil war', *World Development* 30 (1), 61–75.

71 See Wallensteen, P. and Sollenberg, M. (2000) 'Armed conflict 1989–99', *Journal of Peace Research*, 37, 635–649.

72 Goodhand, J. (2003) op. cit., p. 629.

73 Collier, P. et al. (2003) op. cit., p. 188.

74 Ibid., p. 641.

Chapter 3

International Experience of Reconstruction

Introduction: defining 'reconstruction'

Where societies are experiencing violent conflict, it has become commonplace for the international community to intervene, either while the conflict is ongoing or, more frequently, in the post-conflict situation. That intervention can take a number of forms, not always in isolation. There can be military intervention, whether multilateral or otherwise – as in Kuwait in 1991 or Somalia in 1992. Secondly, there can be humanitarian intervention, part of the justification of military intervention in Kosovo in 1998. Thirdly, and usually after the initial military or crisis humanitarian intervention phase is passed, there is intervention to rebuild the war-torn society.

'Reconstruction', as this international intervention has become known, is now a major global concern. It involves individual governments through their departments (such as the Department for International Development (DFID) in the UK, or the Department of Foreign Affairs in Ireland). There are, in addition, major international bodies with the backing of a multiplicity of governments, most notable being the UN and the EU. The former acts as an umbrella for numerous organisations involved in reconstruction in one way or another – from the World Bank to the UNHCR. The EU's efforts in this area are channelled through the European Agency for Reconstruction. Finally, reconstruction has involved the efforts of many development NGOs, both national and international – such as Trócaire and Goal in Ireland, Oxfam and the Catholic Institute for International Relations in the United Kingdom – and human rights organisations such as International Alert in London, Human Rights Watch in New York, the War-torn Societies Project in Geneva, and Women Waging Peace in London and New York.

Given that, as we shall see in Chapter 6, the international community became involved in Ireland in the aftermath of the republican and loyalist cease-fires of 1994 – most notably the EU with its programme for peace and reconciliation – it is necessary to examine in this chapter the ways in which these international bodies have approached the question of reconstruction.

While the word 'reconstruction' is used widely in relation to post-conflict societies, it is evident that there is a range of interpretations of its meaning. At the extremes of the debate are two 'camps', the one arguing for a narrowly economic approach, the other stressing the essential role of social and political policies. At times there would appear to be agreement over definitions – for example, the widespread acceptance of the role of 'civil society' in peace-building, or the importance of enhancing 'social capital', and the somewhat less widespread acknowledgement that human rights and justice are essential elements of reconstruction. However, some of that agreement is more apparent than real. While the analysis or critique of one 'camp' has at times influenced the other to expand its argument, the appearance of consensus is frequently due to one of two factors: first, the dominance of one camp's discourse, whereby the use of the common language signifies less agreement than a passport to acceptance at the debating table, even more pointedly, the *sine qua non* of seeking funding; second, the use of common terms, but with radically different meanings.

This chapter will therefore look critically at the economic approach to reconstruction as evident in some of the programmes of the World Bank. It will then consider the wider approach espoused by international NGOs. Such an approach focuses, among other issues, on human rights, dealing with the human rights abuses of the past, demobilisation of combatants, as well as the specific needs of women, children and young people. It also has crucial points to make in relation to the principles underlying the funding of reconstruction. Finally, the chapter will examine the apparent common ground between the two approaches, and in particular the insistence on 'civil society' and 'social capital'.

Economic reconstruction

Neo-liberal intervention

While violent political conflicts rage or in their immediate aftermath, it is common that the only sort of intervention that is possible, especially on the part of the international community, is an emergency one. Widespread destruction, displacement of populations, and famine require humanitarian responses. Such was the case in places like Tigray[1] and Afghanistan; for example, in relation to Afghanistan, the International Crisis Group judged that the priorities were 'rebuilding shattered infrastructure and clearing the mines'.[2]

Frequently, these early interventions also focus overwhelmingly on issues of security as the prerequisite for further intervention. To take Afghanistan again as an example, DFID's conclusion was that: 'The key to achieving Afghanistan's reform objectives, and those of the international community, is establishing security and law and order across the country.'[3]

Once the humanitarian needs and security issues have been settled, or at least contained, the next stage is to consider the longer-term reconstruction of the war-torn society. It is at this point that the division between the two approaches identified above becomes apparent.

For organisations such as the World Bank, the starting point for intervention is that 'reconstruction' has a very specific meaning – the rebuilding of infrastructure and political and economic institutions in the aftermath of violent political conflict. 'Much of the Bank's work in post-conflict reconstruction over the past decade has been in rebuilding physical infrastructure such as roads and buildings – a traditional area of strength …'[4] At one level this focus is logical given that such work is often the most obvious priority in war-torn societies. As the World Bank concludes: 'It is easier to rebuild roads and bridges than it is to reconstruct institutions and strengthen the social fabric of a society'.[5]

Thus in the Democratic Republic of the Congo, a society ravaged by a complex set of wars, the consequences of which have left millions dead and widespread social disorder, the World Bank's Country Director, Emmanual Mbi, stressed that economic reform was the only item on the Bank's agenda for the reconstruction of the region: 'The Bank's early engagement was meant to convey the message that the "international community has the obligation to respond to a government that puts together a responsible and sound economic reform program ...".'[6]

Similarly, in Afghanistan, World Bank assistance focused on four areas: job generation, strengthening fiscal strategy, reform of public administration, and encouragement of growth of the private sector.[7]

But there is more than merely an emergency response to crisis involved; for example, as the Bank's report on Palestine conveys, there is a political agenda which requires the Bank to focus on economic reconstruction without explicitly entering the minefield of ongoing political conflict. '... by providing comprehensive yearly reports on the state of the Palestinian economy and the emerging financial needs, *strictly limited to the economic realm,* the organisation has maintained *its image of impartiality'* [emphases added].[8]

Of course impartiality is a chimera in such politically charged situations. The World Bank has an agenda, that of bringing the society concerned into the global world of neo-liberalism and 'open markets'. As Moore puts it, '... the Bank's prime concern is not with the causes of conflict and the war itself, but in positioning itself ... "to be able to respond to the challenge of investing".'[9] Nor is the World Bank alone in this regard. An almost religious belief in the conflict-solving powers of neo-liberalism is common in many major international institutions which enter societies coming out of war. Thus the US-based Center for Strategic and International Studies urged that in Iraq: 'Idle hands must be put to work ...' What that means in practical terms is that the US and other states involved in the reconstruction of Iraq '... must get a large number of formerly state-owned enterprises up and running. Even if many of them are not competitive *and may need to be privatised and downsized eventually*, now is the time to get as many people back to work as possible' [emphases added].[10] In other words, the long-term objective is the establishment in Iraq of a capitalist economy built on neo-liberal principles – investment, profit, market forces – rather than commitment to the more nebulous principle of the right to work. As a white Zimbabwean businessman in Mozambique put it: 'The investor who gets in while the bullets are still flying is the man who makes a bundle.'[11]

Poverty reduction

The World Bank claims that poverty reduction is at the core of its work. The first sentence of the Bank's mission statement reads: 'The World Bank Group's mission is to fight poverty and improve the living standards of people in the developing world'.[12] One of the main criticisms made of the narrow approach to reconstruction is that a focus solely on economic reconstruction does not necessarily lessen poverty. This is not to say that no one benefits from economic reconstruction. In the immediate phase of post-war rebuilding of infrastructure, the benefits to transnational capital are glaringly apparent, as the experience of US firms Halliburton and Bechtel in Iraq currently makes clear.[13] And in the longer term, as radical critics point out,[14] the neo-liberal policies, such as structural adjustment, imposed by the World Bank and the International Monetary Fund, serve to incorporate less developed economies and thereby contribute to the profits of stronger western and northern economies. At the same time, the poor of less developed countries are frequently further impoverished as the market is given free rein. The facts thus do not confirm the claim that economic development benefits all.

In addition, by focusing on economic or financial measures, organisations such as the World Bank frequently fail to recognise the potential for conflict transformation and peace-building. For example, the World Bank opposed the 'arms-for-land' programme in El Salvador. By standard economic measures it was not a spectacular programme, but given the fact that conflict over land was central to the violence in El Salvador, the contribution of the programme to attacking the root causes of conflict was significant. It helped establish the peace upon which economic development could be built.[15]

Much of this global debate about development and reconstruction may seem far removed from the concerns of post-1998 Agreement/cease-fire Ireland. In a chronic low-level conflict such as existed in Ireland the destruction of infrastructure was much less than in most other war-torn societies. At the same time, one immediate consequence of the cease-fires of 1994 was a major intervention by the EU with a programme for peace and reconciliation. The extent to which the EU followed a straightforward neo-liberal philosophy in terms of reconstruction in Ireland or, alternatively, adopted a fuller approach, one involving commitment to social and political reconstruction, will be the focus of Chapter 6. But first we need to examine in detail the characteristics of this alternative approach to reconstruction before assessing the common ground, if any, between the two philosophies that inspire intervention internationally.

Social and political reconstruction

In South Africa the victims' support group Khulumani is currently working with US lawyer Michael Hausfeld to bring a class action under the US Alien Tort Claims Act on behalf of approximately 90 victims of apartheid who suffered human rights abuses – rape, torture, etc. – under the previous regime. They are accusing 22 transnational companies – such as BP, Barclays, and IBM – of knowingly supporting apartheid. This ground-breaking legal action is opposed by, among others, Leon Lowe, the Executive Director of the South Africa Free Market Foundation, who argues:

> The only thing you can do ultimately for people is to become rich. The country has to become prosperous. And all of this messing about is actually retarding the prospect of that happening which in the end harms the intended beneficiaries, ordinary black South Africans.[16]

In this stark difference of opinion is encapsulated the clash between the approach to reconstruction of many international NGOs and that of organisations such as the World Bank, which we have considered above. It is to the approach of the international NGOs that we will now turn.

Human rights

The emphasis in the approach to reconstruction by a wide range of international NGOs is on rebuilding the fabric of society with a clear commitment to humanitarian ideals and social rights. For such organisations, this commitment applies even at the earliest stages of conflict transformation. Thus, while SFOR in Bosnia-Herzegovina or US and British troops in Iraq may prioritise security, INGOs stress that genuine security results less from superior fire-power than from a commitment to human rights. As Rory Mungoven, Global Advocacy Director of Human Rights Watch, states: 'Lesson number one from Afghanistan is that, without security there will be no reconstruction. Lesson number two is that without protecting human rights, there will be no genuine security either.'[17] Kenneth Roth, Executive Director of the Human Rights Watch, made the same point in a letter to G8 leaders prior to the Evian-les-Bains summit to discuss reconstruction in Iraq: '… human rights protection is central to successful reconstruction efforts …' What that means in practice is very specific. 'As has been learned in Afghanistan, Iraq's transition will be fatally compromised unless basic security is established, and those officials with a record of human rights abuse are removed from positions of power and influence.'[18] In fact, such an approach involves a redefinition of the standard western interventionist view of security. For Human Rights Watch, genuine security is not about tanks and guns, but about establishing respect for the rule of law and human rights. Genuine security requires commitment to police reforms, establishment of human rights institutions, an independent judiciary, the retraining of lawyers and an internationally led process to account for past human rights abuses.[19]

For Oxfam, the same lesson emerges from consideration of the violent conflict in the Great Lakes region of Africa. Reconstruction entails justice, which includes international efforts to end impunity, the reform of the judiciary, punishment for extra-judicial killings, and bringing criminals to the International Criminal Tribunal for Rwanda.[20]

Dealing with the past

There is a consistent message coming from the international experience that some formal mechanism for coming to terms with past human rights abuses is essential in reconstruction. As the War-Torn Societies Project puts it: 'The restoration of justice by itself does not heal relations …' Societies coming out of war need to do more than prosecute offenders; they need to recognise that formal 'truth and historical verification commissions can play an important role.'[21]

Dealing with the past through the formal mechanism of a truth commission is a strategy that has been chosen in more than 20 countries in the last three decades.[22] In each case, the expectation was that the commission could deal with the unfinished business of human rights abuses in the previous regime: issues such as impunity, where the armed forces escaped prosecution for murder, torture, disappearances, etc.; the distortion of the rule of law whereby it became another weapon against political dissent; the suspension or emasculation of means whereby victims could, in principle, seek justice, such as trials, inquests, etc.

Frequently, victims have approached these truth commissions with a mixture of euphoria and trepidation. The establishment of a commission seems to hold out the promise of the truth about the past finally being revealed. The hope is that the shell of impunity is finally cracked, forcing perpetrators to acknowledge the wrongs they have done, and perhaps even apologise to victims. In the end, as most notably in the South African Truth and Reconciliation Commission, the goal is, as its title reveals, to bring about reconciliation in a post-conflict, traumatised society.

Unfortunately, the experience is that the reality usually falls far short of the promise. Truth commissions are often limited in their scope, confined to a certain class of abuse or a specific period of the past; even then, they are time-limited, required to report in what often turns out to be too short a time. Perpetrators may find ways to avoid appearing, or to be economical with the truth when they do so. They may not apologise and there may ultimately be no reconciliation. That said, they have become a popular device, with the result that pressure to establish such a mechanism in a transitional society can often come not merely from victims within the society but also from the international community. International NGO involvement was central in the establishment of the truth commission in Rwanda[23] and currently in Sierra Leone.[24] UN involvement was central in the establishment of the truth commission in El Salvador.[25] And with international intervention also came external funding.

There is room for ambivalence in relation to assessing the global popularity of truth commissions: even the least successful can serve to send out powerful symbolic messages at home and abroad about the rejection of the past and the hope of establishing a culture of human rights in the future. As Ignatieff puts it, they 'narrow the range of permissible lies'.[26]

At the same time, most truth commissions have been fashioned in such a way as not to radically challenge the global agenda of neo-liberalism. This was clear already in one of the earliest truth commissions, that in Chile, where the report revealed state involvement in murder and disappearance without investigating US involvement in the overthrow of the democratically elected government of Salvador Allende.[27]

One measure of whether dealing with the past is taken seriously by the transitional society and the international community is the extent to which there is a willingness to go beyond a one-off commission. Many victims groups in societies which have had a formal truth mechanism have found that many of their questions remain unanswered because the commission has not had enough time, authority or finances. Yet they are expected to now turn the page and move on.

Similarly, INGOs are critical of the piecemeal approach of many international interventions in societies coming out of conflict. Oxfam has argued that the secret to successful reconstruction is the coordination of efforts. They provide a list of the kinds of policies that would follow from such 'joined up' thinking. For example, transnational corporations should be concerned about human rights rather than solely with the pursuit of markets or profits; new aid should not be used for debt payments; and demobilization of combatants and decommissioning of arms is useless unless linked to a campaign against continuing arms sales. And in a position which dramatically expands that of organisations such as the World Bank, Oxfam states that the purpose of investment in post-conflict societies is to 'reduce poverty, avoid conflict and promote human rights'. Thus, transnational corporations must be required to follow internationally accepted social and environmental standards.[28]

Oxfam's focus on transnational corporations is an interesting one, frequently overlooked in societies coming out of conflict. Another INGO, International Alert, has spelt out in greater detail what a human-rights based approach might entail for transnational corporations. At a minimum, it would require compliance with national regulations and internationally agreed laws, conventions and standards. A medium strategy would involve transnational corporations being aware of their ability to create or exacerbate conflict; they should seek, therefore, to 'do no harm' through their actions. There is also a maximum strategy, which involves the transnational corporation in a proactive contribution to peace-building through social investment, stakeholder consultation, policy dialogue, advocacy and civil institution building. Specifically, this would require the transnational corporation to become involved not only in the obvious tasks of investing in productive sectors, but also in more imaginative areas such as a focus on projects that target affected populations and ex-combatants, support for NGOs active in reconciliation efforts, voter education, etc., and participation in truth and reconciliation commissions.[29]

Of course, much of this literature relates to societies very different from Ireland, not least in terms of levels of economic development. Despite that, there is immediate resonance to the Irish situation where the peace process has led to a number of promises and expectations in relation to human rights. We will examine the extent to which the promises have been delivered and the expectations realised in depth in Chapter 6.

Demobilisation

Reconstruction frequently involves activities that are not normal development activities, such as: delivery of emergency aid; disarmament and demobilisation of former combatants and their reintegration into society; resettlement of displaced people; repatriation of foreign troops; reform of the armed forces and of the civilian police; establishment of a framework for national reconciliation, e.g. a truth commission; economic reconstruction; reconstruction of basic services; and clearance of mines.[30]

Of these, it is argued that the single most important is 'the successful disarmament, demobilisation, repatriation, resettlement and reintegration of former combatants'. '... while it might be costly, long-term costs for society ... could be larger if the ex-combatants were unable to find new livelihoods' – increased unemployment, rising crime rate, political instability. More positively, ex-combatants have skills to offer communities and society as a whole.[31]

It should go without saying that not all combatants are male. Yet it is clear that in many cases of demobilisation, the specific needs of female combatants have not been taken into consideration.

> ... female ex-combatants, as well as other women in war-affected communities, had usually acquired new roles during the war, and after the war were often expected by men to return to their traditional roles. This has created considerable tensions. A high divorce rate has for example been observed between ex-fighters in Eritrea.[32]

In Eritrea, as elsewhere, 'society does not always show sympathy towards the female ex-fighters when they refuse to return to the traditional role and submissive behaviour expected of them.'[33]

It follows that the political objective is the most important one in reconstruction. If there is a conflict between the objective of restoring peace and that of development more widely defined, the former must be selected. 'Because peace is a precondition for sustainable development, economic priorities should always be guided by political considerations.'[34]

Specifically, the reintegration of former combatants should not be determined by economic or financial considerations. Financial constraints on demobilisation are what almost derailed the peace process in El Salvador, led to the collapse of peace building in Angola, caused serious setbacks to the transition in Cambodia, and served to spread the conflict from Kosovo to neighbouring countries. Demobilisation must be supported even if the overall process of stabilising the economy and revitalising economic growth are delayed.

That said, the global experience of demobilisation reveals starkly differing levels of success. In South Africa, for example, an important factor in the rise of post-conflict crime has been the inability of ex-combatants, especially from guerrilla forces, to acquire jobs and reasonable income.[35] Experts and NGOs working on demobilisation agree that perhaps the most important lesson in terms of success is self-help. For example, Berdal argues: '... community-based vocational training programmes aimed at developing practical skills for self-employment, administered by ex-combatants themselves ... and/or NGOs, have shown the greatest promise of success both in terms of cost-effectiveness and by reducing the potential for political tensions'.[36]

He elaborates on this point as follows:

> One reason for the relative success of community-based programmes, especially involving veterans, is that they are more sensitive to local needs and, on the basis of the limited evidence that does exist, appear not only to offer more flexibility, but also to be better geared towards integrating ex-combatants and their dependants into society. At the same time, the results of community-based initiatives are more easily monitored, and corrective action more easily taken, than with large-scale, centralised and state-managed programmes. These, by contrast, have proved ill-suited for short-to-medium-term reintegration efforts.[37]

An interesting comparison in this regard is that of Eritrea and Ethiopia. In Eritrea ex-combatants had long experience of building the new society in liberated zones during the conflict. Having won the war of liberation, they saw their demobilisation as an integral part of the development of their society and applied the same skills of self-organisation and self-help in that process. They received little outside financial support in demobilisation; 10 per cent of the total cost of demobilisation and reintegration came from external assistance.[38] In Ethiopia on the other hand, 65 per cent of the cost of demobilisation and reintegration came from external assistance, but the programme is acknowledged as having been less successful than in Eritrea. The ex-combatants in this case were government troops, ex-soldiers who had in effect failed in their career as soldiers.[39] They continued to rely on the state to organise their reintegration and had little previous experience of self-help or community development.

Much of this has direct relevance to the Irish experience where ex-prisoners groups have worked on the demobilisation of former combatants inspired by self-help and community development logic with limited financial support from external funders or the state. This will be examined in Chapter 6.

Women

Over the past decade there has been increasing recognition that a 'gender-blind' approach to conflict resolution and reconstruction has been a critical element in the global failure to achieve a sustainable peace.

Thus the exclusion of women from the UN-organised, -facilitated and -sponsored peace conferences in Somalia helped to enhance the legitimacy of the warlords, who are often strangers in local communities.[40] The exclusion of women from peace conferences has had discernible and quantifiable adverse consequences, for women in particular, but also for their families and for their societies, in examples drawn from the Ivory Coast, Sierra Leone and Angola.[41]

Although women have, on rare occasions, emerged empowered from the experience of war, it is more usual to find women losing what has been a hard-won autonomy once war ends. Cockburn phrases this in stark terms:

> ... the civil society rebuilt after war or tyranny seldom reflects women's visions or rewards their energies. The space that momentarily opens up for change is not often used to secure genuine and lasting gender transformations. Effort may be put into healing enmity by reshaping ethnic and national relations, but gender and class relations are usually allowed to revert to the status quo ante. Old privileges may be in eclipse, but a new business elite, a new criminal underworld, a reformed police service come into being as the familiar masculinity hierarchies ... Instead of the skills and confidence forged by some women by the furnace of war being turned to advantage, the old sexual division of labour is reconstituted, in the family, in the labour force.[42]

As the South African experience, to name but one, indicates, resisting ideologies that assert women's 'proper role' to be primarily domestic remains an important and potentially conflictual issue in a period of social reconstruction.[43]

The growing acceptance of the necessity to incorporate the skills and perspectives of women as well as men, not only into the task of peace-making, but also within technical assistance projects, peace-keeping activities and reconstruction after conflict, is based in part upon principles of justice, democracy and human rights but also upon empirical research that the increased participation of women can 'make a difference'.

Without essentialising women's role as 'peacemakers', there is sufficient evidence to demonstrate that their contribution to peace-making has been considerable.[44] Interviews with Bosnian women, five years after the war, showed that women who were looked after at women's centres suffered much less from post-traumatic stress than women who did not receive help.[45] Rwanda leads the world in terms of the inclusion of women in national parliaments (49 per cent), with women occupying 32 per cent of cabinet places, including portfolios in justice, lands, economic planning, primary and secondary education. Rwandan women are also heavily involved in other areas in the process of reconstruction, such as human rights courts, their participation testimony to the crucial contribution women can make to rebuilding a society based on human rights.[46]

The organisation Women Waging Peace has summed up women's global contribution:

> Women have their fingers on the pulse of the community and can gather essential information on the ground to mobilise post-conflict reconciliation and reconstruction ... Women foster confidence and trust among local populations, since they often care for the maimed, injured and orphaned. They propose constructive solutions while suggesting innovative approaches for dialogue among polarised groups. They sometimes use unorthodox means such as singing and dancing to diffuse potentially violent situations.[47]

Gender balance, in terms of the active and equal participation of women in peace processes and in all areas of decision-making, is an essential part of reconstruction. But while reconstruction efforts that simply target women and their needs may alleviate the worst of the burden, they do not challenge women's subordinate position. Until male gender roles are also scrutinised and challenged, women will not achieve meaningful equality. This does not 'remove the need or desirability for women-specific programmes or projects.'[48] But, at the same time, as the UN puts it, the ultimate goal is 'to ensure equal rights, responsibilities and opportunities of women and men, and girls and boys.' The strategy used to achieve this objective is gender mainstreaming, namely:

> ... a strategy for making women's concerns as well as men's concerns and experiences an integral dimension in the design, implementation, monitoring and evaluation of policies and programmes in all political, economic and social spheres so that women and men benefit equally and inequality is not perpetuated.[49]

The impetus for global efforts to advance the status of women can be traced to the Nairobi Conference of 1975, which marked the opening of the UN International Decade for Women. The equal participation of women in efforts to achieve equality, peace and development were adopted as overriding themes. Building on this, the Convention on the Elimination of Discrimination Against Women (CEDAW), formulated by the UN General Assembly in 1979, encourages affirmative action measures to ensure women's equal participation in political and public life. While this has been ratified by 168 countries to date, the failure by many to ratify the Optional Protocol means that individual women cannot make a complaint against their government for breaches of CEDAW.[50] However, governments are required to submit periodic reports detailing their progress towards the goals set by CEDAW.

At the Fourth World Conference on Women in Beijing in 1995 it was agreed that unless women's perspectives were incorporated at all levels of decision-making, 'the goals of equality, development and peace cannot be achieved.' At Beijing, governments made a voluntary commitment to implement a Platform for Action to promote the advancement of women in twelve agreed *Critical Areas of Concern*.[51]

By 2000, efforts by a number of organisations, including the Women's International League for Peace and Freedom and International Alert, to put pressure on the global community to implement effective policy led to Security Council Resolution 1325, 'a watershed political framework' in the words of UNIFEM, to ensure the inclusion of women in all aspects of peace-building and political life.

> ... understanding of the impact of armed conflict on women and girls, effective institutional arrangements to guarantee their protection and full participation in the peace process can significantly contribute to the maintenance and promotion of international peace and security.[52]

The non-political and invisible nature of 'the private' may explain a reluctance within the field of conflict management to address the 'gendered' and somehow 'natural' features of armed conflict, like domestic violence and rape. There is an urgent need to examine the links between this 'private' violence and the 'public' violence of armed conflict:

> The attitudes and values that give rise to the former lay the ground work for the latter. Both are rooted in mindsets where domination, control and beliefs in certain groups' superiority and others' inferiority are central.

> A mind set that permits and justifies the use of physical
> or psychological force by a 'superior' against an 'inferior'
> cannot be safely relegated to one corner of life, such as
> the home, or certain personal relationships. It will
> become a part of public life.[53]

As the experiences of the organisation Kvinna Till Kvinna in
many different zones of conflict make plain, the post-war
rebuilding process also requires a change in attitudes.

> If nationalism and prejudice are allowed to flourish then
> conflicts will easily rise to the surface again. In most
> societies affected by war and hostilities the gender roles
> are very conservative. The key to sustainable peace
> could therefore lie in changing stereotype gender roles
> and improving gender equality within the various sections
> of the community.[54]

In 1993 the UN General Assembly passed Resolution 48/104,
specifically on violence against women, reaffirming that
violence is a violation of women's fundamental human rights.
A number of international and regional declarations and
campaigns on violence against women have reiterated this
sentiment and urged societies to raise awareness on the
issue; criminalise all forms of gender-based violence; build
capacities and empower women to speak out about
experiences of violence; build indicators and collect data
highlighting the prevalence of such violence; adopt 'best
practice' to eliminate gender-based violence.[55]

This debate is highly relevant in terms of the transition from
violent conflict in Northern Ireland. Rising levels of gender-
based violence against women are occurring[56] and pose
worrying questions for the construction of a post-conflict
society.

A sustainable base for future conflict prevention will not be achieved without the examination of discourses around masculinity. Men's identities 'may emerge more damaged from a period of conflict and if during reconstruction no attention is paid to alternative positive masculinities in opposition to essentialist masculinity, the reassertion of traditional gender norms and roles is inevitable.'[57] Existing patterns of entrenched masculinity are unlikely to change without the increased representation and participation of women. '... a framework of peacebuilding and reconstruction must address socially entrenched gender-based discrimination.'[58] As Myrttinen puts it, the groundwork for a sustainable peace must begin with a 'gendered analysis of the situation', so that a reduction in weapons would be 'coupled with a "demobilisation" of the militarised, violent concepts of masculinity that would see a weapons collection process as "emasculating"'.[59]

The empowerment of women to participate in decision-making should go alongside the empowerment of men as parents, carers and community workers.

Despite the improved international rhetoric, it is clear that all too often reconstruction priorities remain dominated by men and male-determined issues. Studies suggest that rights-based concerns must be attended to prior to reconstruction, 'otherwise post-conflict pressures to resume the status quo may lead to reconstruction plans becoming fixed by earlier prevailing gender norms, and the opportunity for societal transformation incorporating human rights to promote gender equity is lost.'[60] But even a late start is better than none. The most effective strategy, country-based evidence suggests, is for the establishment of a broad-based human rights framework with women's equal rights guaranteed as part of the national commitment to non-discrimination. This can provide long-term gains more successfully than simply singling out women's rights as a specific group.

In post-conflict situations, the aim of governments must be to recast social, political and economic bases of power in order to achieve human security. Conceptualisations of 'security' have expanded considerably, most notably in the influential report of Ogata and Sen for the *Commission on Human Security*, which begins from the premise that achieving human security must include not only protection but a strategy to empower people to fend for themselves. This has particular resonances when considered in gendered terms. Female-headed households are particularly prevalent in post-conflict situations, due to death, imprisonment and dislocation of male partners. Much of women's work tends to be outside the market, without formal financial compensation, performing basic but critical activities such as child rearing and elder care. While such roles improve economic security at a household level and are vital in terms of the stability of society, this work is often not recognised and not valued. Empowering women with livelihoods is important for their economic security, while in the longer-term the fact of employment 'catalyzes change in attitudes towards women that alone can lead to enduring empowerment.'[61] Reproductive health is also vital in ensuring the human security of women as, in addition to improving the security of their children and families, it gives women the means of deciding the numbers of children they wish to bear. Reproductive health must be seen in conjunction with education for girls and women as fundamental to health, to the reduction of fertility rates and to the overall well-being of families. For example, in Ghana, children of educated mothers are twice as likely to survive to their fifth birthday as children of uneducated mothers.[62]

The feminisation of poverty 'is not simply about the numbers of women who are poor but also encompasses understanding of the gendered ways in which women fall into poverty and its consequences for them.' Ways in which women become impoverished include widowhood, lack of paid employment and low paid, irregular employment, the consequences of domestic violence and legal restrictions on the ownership of property.[63] Understanding the gender dimension of poverty illustrates why women-specific programmes continue to be necessary.

Thus there are compelling arguments for the incorporation of gender analysis in economic policies, for more gender-specific data and gender-sensitive analysis,[64] and for the introduction by government of 'gender budgets'. [65] Research has demonstrated that improvements in the economic position of women tend to have more positive effects for children and other members of the household than improvements in men's income.[66]

Major international organisations have been at the forefront of the incorporation of gender in approaches to development and reconstruction. For example, the Organisation for Economic Development and Cooperation (OECD) Development Assistance Committee (DAC) established guidelines in 1998, focusing on gender equality and women's empowerment and emphasising the participation of women and men as necessary to processes of peace-building and development. A 2001 supplement to the OECD-DAC guidelines is testimony to the growing sophistication in thinking on the role of gender in conflict-reduction strategies.

The DAC now calls for greater inclusion in peace-building of the skills and initiatives women have demonstrated 'that reflect collaboration and the principle of community action across ethnic, religious, linguistic and other divides.'[67] The G8 leaders also recognise the roles played by women and have stressed the importance of:

> ... full and equal participation in all phases of conflict prevention, resolution, and peacebuilding; demobilisation and reintegration programmes that consider the specific needs of female ex-combatants and their dependents; gender sensitive training for all members of peace-related operations; inclusion of women in operational posts at all levels; and integration of a gender perspective and women's participation in the development, design, implementation, monitoring and evaluation of bilateral and multilateral assistance programs.[68]

Even the World Bank has highlighted the role of women in rebuilding social capital, 'calling for attention to their potential as strong community leaders who can facilitate the rebuilding process.'[69]

Children and young people

Even more ignored in the international literature is the effect of war on young people and the consequent need to involve them in reconstruction. While recognition that civilians, including children, bear the brunt of contemporary armed conflicts is now well established, '... there has been relatively little focus on the impact on older boys and girls'.[70]

> In the eyes of the international community, which has reached tremendous heights of political consensus

around the subject of 'innocent, vulnerable, children', adolescents are woefully overlooked. In fact, for many decision-makers, adolescents do not seem like children at all, almost do not exist at all. They seem more like adults, able to care for themselves, or having more adult-like problems. And they may not look so innocent; they may be the perpetrators of violence … Yet the costs of not focusing on adolescents are enormous: massive rights violations committed against adolescents, with long-term consequences for them and their communities as they attempt to endure and recover from armed conflict. Perhaps worst of all, adolescents' strengths and potential as constructive contributors to their societies go largely unrecognised and unsupported by the international community, while those who seek to do them harm, such as by recruiting them into military service or involving them in criminal activity, recognise and utilise their capabilities very well.[71]

Particular risks for young people include the following:[72] compared to younger children, they are more likely to be recruited into military service, to attend school in far fewer numbers (this is especially true for adolescent girls), to be sexually abused or abducted and held as sexual slaves; they also run a higher risk of contracting HIV/AIDS and other sexually transmitted infections and are the least likely of all displaced persons to access health-care services. At the same time they may be required to head households after the loss of parents or in other ways assume adult responsibilities without sufficient support. Above all, they are seldom asked for their opinions.

All too often young people are seen as a cause for concern. Moral panics lead to control interventions rather than attempts to incorporate young people. This tendency is heightened in a post-conflict situation. Hence the timely call of an International Young Parliament in 2003 for a focus on restorative justice rather than criminal justice approaches to young people involved in conflict.[73]

There are thus sound reasons for paying much more attention to the needs and potential of young people in reconstruction. In addition, there is an international framework available which allows more intervention, including the Convention on the Rights of the Child, the *Impact of Armed Conflict on Children* study (Machel Report),[74] and the UN Secretary-General's Special Representative for Children and Armed Conflict. And, ultimately, there are sound political reasons for this focus too. As one group has remarked in relation to one conflict zone, Sierra Leone, there is a need:

> to place young people's concerns and their capacities at the center of recovery efforts. Recognising that they were at the center of the war, they believe they must be at the center of peacemaking and reconstruction. Without better support and respect for their rights, young people will become more angry and disaffected, and are likely to become a major source of new unrest.[75]

There are undoubtedly lessons for Ireland from the international experience. All too often it seems that the approach to young people is simply one of silence or condemnation. Questions need to be asked about the extent to which the needs of children and young people have been put at the centre of conflict transformation. The record to date will be examined in Chapter 6.

Funding conflict transformation

Much of what passes for reconstruction carried out by international organisations such as the World Bank falls woefully short of the ideal of conflict transformation. Goodhand and Atkinson focus on one phenomenon already mentioned in Chapter 2, conditionality – the crude attempt to link political and humanitarian responses through the policy of aid. In Afghanistan, for example, prior to the overthrow of the Taliban, financial support for water and sanitation projects in Kabul was dependent on enhancing democratic and human rights. Apart from being ethically problematic, there was little evidence that this approach changed Taliban behaviour in any way.[76] History repeated itself when US forces in Afghanistan in May 2004 distributed leaflets calling on people to provide information on al-Qaida and the Taliban at the risk of losing humanitarian aid.[77]

Likewise, in Liberia, the policy of conditional aid proved to be a blunt instrument which impacted more on the general population than on politicians. In this situation, the authors conclude, what was needed was 'more positive action on the ground, including political engagement (and not just negative conditionalities) and the provision of resources for rehabilitation and development'.[78]

In Sri Lanka, according to the authors, the problem was not so much a crude interpretation of conditionality than the fact that the World Bank introduced a structural adjustment and economic liberalisation package that failed to take account of the local historical and political context. An approach which took the issue of conflict seriously and mainstreamed it in its policy and programmes would have led, at least, to a balance between liberalisation and social investment, between support for the state and support for civil society. Specifically, policies would have been very different if the World Bank had viewed the Sri Lanka conflict as a crisis of the state rather than an ethnic conflict.

The conclusion is that in all three societies, donors emphasised doing rather than understanding. They did not adapt to local conditions. There was no contextual analysis nor any attempt to take conflict seriously into account in funding decisions. As a result, the donors dealt with the most powerful (usually armed) groups in each situation, and ignored the grass roots.

Above all, the shortcoming of these mainstream approaches has been the failure to take community development seriously. 'Civil society groups tended to be marginalised by peace processes. Peacemakers have often failed to look beyond the peace accord'.[79] Donor involvement with civil society is often naïve and ham-fisted:

> Donor agencies have a natural tendency to focus on the short-term and the easily measurable and therefore tend to concentrate on the physical infrastructure of civil society ... Few have attempted to move beyond projectised approaches into supporting strategies and processes.[80]

In short, all too often the main approach has been to work *around* or *in* conflict. Very few work *on* conflict. There are few examples to be found in practice of peace-building/ conflict transformation being mainstreamed by major donor agencies such as the World Bank; they are happier with stand-alone, projectised approaches. Worse, 'by creating a separate sphere called conflict transformation and peacebuilding, which is delinked from issues like justice and democratisation, politics and power are leached out of the process. Peacebuilding, therefore, is depoliticised'.[81]

In addition, more caution is creeping into the funding process. 'Funding levels are decreasing while the conditions attached to aid are growing. This is not an environment that is conducive to experimentation and innovation.'[82]

Again the relevance of the international debate on funding to the specifics of the Irish context is apparent. Since the 1994 cease-fires, two major European Programmes, Peace I and Peace II, have channelled large amounts of money into Northern Ireland and the Border region of Ireland. The first of these came closer to matching the ideals of conflict transformation laid out above, while the second has moved away from the ideals identified globally as conducive to conflict transformation and reconstruction. The Irish situation will be examined in detail in Chapter 6.

Common ground?

Neo-liberalism and social reconstruction

Recently it has become possible to find criticism of the narrow approach to reconstruction, albeit muted, even in World Bank circles. Thus the World Bank country manager in East Timor, Elisabeth Huybens, noted the 'difficulty in striking a balance between meeting the immediate needs on the ground in the face of destruction, whilst keeping in mind longer term development concerns. We now see that the sectors in which we worked more slowly, in the context of a framework that had a long-term vision and strategy, are the ones that have been most successful'.[83]

The World Bank has displayed an interest in 'post-conflict reconstruction' from 1993 when its Operational Policy on Development Cooperation and Conflict mandated the integration of sensitivity to conflict in Bank assistance through conflict analysis. In the five years following 1993, the World Bank gave out $400 million in grants to post-conflict societies.[84] In 1997, they established their Post-Conflict Unit which has a sophisticated model for judging the potential for violent conflict in societies where they are involved, the Conflict Analysis Framework.[85] This framework argues that there are six key factors influencing conflict: social and ethnic relations; governance and political institutions; *human rights and security*; economic structure and performance; environment and natural resources; external factors [emphasis added].

The acknowledgement that even as financially and technically oriented an organisation as the World Bank must take the issue of conflict transformation seriously is captured in a key finding of this report: 'At worst, conflict-blind development assistance may inadvertently exacerbate conflict; at best, it may simply be irrelevant to the issues that force many of a country's citizens into a situation of violent conflict.'[86]

However, this is far short of a full-blooded NGO-style commitment to social reconstruction, as the definitive World Bank statement on its role in post-conflict situations clearly reveals: 'There is a need for capacity to promote economic adjustment and recovery, to address social sector needs, and to build institutional capacity.'[87] The document has nothing to say about past human rights abuses or promoting a future culture of human rights. Nor is there any sense that the Bank is committed to supporting grass-roots organisations or placing genuine community development at the centre of reconstruction programmes. Instead, there is the timid suggestion that 'where security conditions and government commitment allow, broad support for reconstruction would include physical reconstruction, economic recovery, institution-building, and social integration, including active participation of the communities themselves in design and implementation'.[88]

The EU, the second largest multilateral donor after the World Bank, reveals greater understanding of the fact that reconstruction is a social as well as an economic process. Since the mid-1990s, the EU has regarded conflict prevention as central to the task of development. This acknowledgement is captured in the Common Foreign and Security Policy (1997), the European Community Humanitarian Office, and the Conflict Prevention Network. As a result, a major critical assessment of EU conflict intervention has noted:

> There is an increasing consensus that development aid should foster structures that are both economically and socially sustainable. Conflict prevention objectives, therefore, should be part of the long-term development strategies which include economic, social, political and environmentally sound development.[89]

Thus it has now become part of the orthodoxy that reconstruction needs to go beyond economic intervention, and it is now *de rigueur* to acknowledge the importance of the role of human rights in reconstruction. The G8 countries, for example, have accepted the Miyazaki Initiatives for Conflict Resolution. While starting from the traditional viewpoint that 'economic and development co-operation has an important part to play in fostering peace and stability', the statement is prefaced by a commitment to human rights:

The G8 confirms that efforts to prevent conflict must be based upon observance of international law including the UN Charter, democracy, *respect for human rights*, the rule of law, good governance, sustainable development, and other fundamental values, which constitute the foundation of international peace and security [emphasis added].[90]

Just as economic growth can bring stability, so peace and democratic stability are 'indispensable pre-conditions for economic growth and sustainable development'. Hence, there is a need to promote the consideration of conflict prevention in development assistance strategies, e.g. reduction of poverty, attacking root causes of conflicts, promotion of democracy, good governance, rule of law, capacity building in administration, including police and prisons, reducing military expenditure.

In a similar vein, the EU acknowledges that:

In contrast to traditional aid, peace-building is centred on participative processes rather than on outputs, is a long-term path dotted with small successes and even more setbacks, and gives priority to (re)building trust and relationships. The project approach of conventional aid is hardly appropriate in this situation as it may impose unrealistic time-frames and assumptions about the relationship between inputs and outcomes, which do not take account of the complexity of conflict and peace processes. Sometimes, it may be more important to sustain the process than to prematurely insist on concrete ends.[91]

Civil society

There would thus seem to be a large element of common ground between the economic reconstuctionists and the social reconstructionists. Nowhere is this more obvious than in the use of a common language, in particular phrases such as 'civil society', 'capacity building' and 'social capital'.

'Civil society' is taken to refer to the fact that '... people meet, communicate and organise in ways that are not established or controlled by the state, nor by kinship and family ties, and with purposes that are driven neither by the power logics of the state nor by market interests'.[92] The promises of civil society are said to rest in the potential to curb the unbridled power of the state while at the same time being a force for moderation: '... the power of the state is limited by the capacity of individuals to organise themselves collectively' and at the same time 'expresses the potential for toleration, for accommodating different worldviews and lifestyles'.[93]

'Social capital' is a concept popularised through the work of Robert Putnam on Italy. He uses it to refer to: '... features of social organisation, such as trust, norms, and networks, that can improve the efficiency of society by facilitating coordinated actions'.[94]

The commonality may be less real than it appears. There are in fact left and right versions of this discourse, with 'social capital' interpreted by those in the INGO community in a different way from those in organisations such as the World Bank. For the former, it is an affirmation of grass-roots collective solidarity and resilience. When used in this context terms such as 'civil society' and 'social capital' point to a commitment to community development. In a post-conflict situation, it is argued, only such a commitment can guarantee sustained peace-building and social inclusion in a way that all the peace-keeping forces and economic restructuring cannot do.

For organisations such as the World Bank, however, there is a different interpretation. At the very least, the grass roots are seen as entirely subordinate to macro-economic needs and plans. The decision to leave them to get on with the things that they are good at – networking, mutual support – is at very least patronising and marginalising; it is the antithesis of community development. Even in the absence of such a view, the focus can be reduced to merely a technical exercise. The uncritical presumption is that building social capital and encouraging civil society can curb the power of the powerful and can breed tolerance, and the measure of success is in purely technical terms – how many networks, how many cross-community meetings, etc. The end result is that the focus on those at the bottom can serve to take attention away from the systems of power and privilege which can determine not only poverty and inequality, but also the potential for social inclusion and peace-building.

Belloni's consideration of the rhetoric of intervention in Bosnia and Herzegovina reveals the important ideological role of the discourse of 'civil society' and 'social capital'. The less than impressive success of reconstruction in Bosnia and Herzegovina, he argues, engendered a 'surge in interest in civil society building'; it 'stems from progressive disillusionment in the use of traditional incentives to foster democratisation and reconciliation ...' At the heart of the international logic is the belief that 'the allocation of funds to civic groups and NGOs seems a more promising approach towards helping create a sphere where moderation, tolerance and the non-violent resolution of conflicts can take hold'.[95]

The end result is that dependence on the international community 'transforms civil society into a set of regulatory agencies that implement donors' changing priorities'.[96] There is the creation of a 'new divide' between those preserving local identity and an internationalising, technocratic, pro-Western clique – '... a transnational cosmopolitan community of like-minded people who speak the same "language" (literally and symbolically) and share an ethos that is degrees removed from territorially based identities'.[97]

> By understanding civil society building as an essentially technical enterprise that lacks a political vision and sidesteps issues deeply embedded in ethno-politics, the international community ... maintains an idealised and unrealistic vision of civil society as an anti-political arena and it perpetuates the status quo of division, fear and latent conflict. Seen in isolation from the state, or rather as an alternative to state-building, local civil society is destined to be dependent upon the international community and its impact on reconciliation and democratisation limited ... civil society development is a last attempt to compensate for the lack of effectiveness of economic incentives and political direction ... Civil society programs are a less expensive alternative to large-scale institutional, economic and political reform, and allow both international donors and local NGOs to sidestep complex political questions ...[98]

And if 'civil society' played its role in the establishment of neo-liberalism in a former socialist society, so 'social capital' can play a similar role in relation to war-torn Africa. Referring to the World Bank's interest in 'post-conflict reconstruction' and its Post-Conflict Unit, Moore notes that, at one level, the Bank's language sounds almost radical, with its emphasis on humanitarian intervention and participatory development. But closer examination reveals that '... many people working in the humanitarian realm equate "development" with "neo-liberalism" almost automatically: it takes some time for an outsider to the humanitarian community to realise that "development" has lost any left-leaning connotations in this discursive area'.[99]

In fact, there is little substance to humanitarianism. For the World Bank, he argues, humanitarian intervention is not about impartiality, but ideological partisanship – getting in on conflicts before they end with 'development aid starter-kits' and establishing a neo-liberal agenda.

Part of this same agenda is the notion of 'social capital'.

> Americans have a hard time dealing with the idea that conflict can be a normal state of affairs, and they try to avoid the idea of states, too. The notion of 'social capital' can hide both. Social capital is, ambiguously, 'trust' and with trust conflict supposedly disappears. Social capital resides in 'civil society' ... and thus the state, the resources it tends to consume and its often uncomfortable monopoly of the 'legitimate' use of force can be wished away ... Thus the causes of conflict do not have to be addressed ... What is of concern is 'the ability to resolve disputes'. By sidestepping the idea of states and other formal institutions, the notion of social capital becomes ethereal: one talks of vague notions like 'participation', the *perception* of 'effort'...[100]

The acceptance of the social capital paradigm:

> signals the hegemony of the linguistic style of
> 'economics': with its use economists can claim expertise
> in areas traditionally out of their zone of speciality, and at
> the same time the 'softer' social scientist can utilise it to
> impress the grant and consultancy gatekeepers of their
> facility with dominant speech acts.[101]

In the neo-liberal world this discourse helps create
dependency. For example, the World Bank concludes that
many less developed societies do not have the social capital
locally to solve conflict. Given that, the onus falls on the
international community. So while the bank gets on with the
big tasks of macroeconomic restructuring, financial 'reform',
'structural adjustment' etc., the lack of local 'implementing
capacity' will require major decentralisation of administration
and support for 'civil society', especially women, 'the
ubiquitous agents of change'.[102]

In the final analysis, concludes Stiefel, the very best that can
be said of international intervention is that, for all the
commitment to the rhetoric of social reconstruction, it does
not contribute significantly to that process.

External actors continue to shy away from the essentially
political nature of the problems and solutions. They continue
to treat rebuilding and relief as a primarily technical exercise,
and to concentrate on the physical and institutional
challenges of rebuilding, neglecting the more important
challenge of mending relations and restoring trust and dignity.
They tend to neglect the political context and ignore the
political, social and psychological impact of their aid. External
actors continue to assure that rebuilding war-torn societies is
a short- to medium-term exercise that can be inserted into

pre-defined bureaucratic plans and timetables. As a result assistance is often time-limited, irregular and inflexible.[103]

Conclusion

These are hard criticisms, but there is another side to the story. Take the involvement of the EU in the reconstruction of the Balkans, East Timor and South Africa. Its approach has been characterised by emphases on civil society, democracy, human rights and the rule of law. For example, the EU has supported the retraining of judges in Montenegro and the Truth and Reconciliation Commission in South Africa. Even more significant is the fact that it is clear from looking at the accounts of the work of the EU's European Agency for Reconstruction (EAR) in the Balkans that its intervention is marked by imagination, flexibility and a healthy dose of self-criticism. Thus, in assessing a housing reconstruction programme in Macedonia, the EAR notes the extent to which the programme has failed in one of its goals, that of persuading refugees and internally displaced people to return to formerly multi-ethnic villages, and concludes that 'house reconstruction could not independently solve, in spite of well intended efforts, the issues of full reconciliation and permanent security'.[104] The European Parliament is proud of the work of EAR in the Balkans and holds it up as a model for EU involvement in the reconstruction of Afghanistan.[105]

Does the foregrounding of conflict transformation, human rights and empowering civil society represent a progressive development, in part inspired by genuine grass-roots demands? Or is it a necessary adjustment to political and social structures to ensure the survival and diffusion of even more neo-liberalism? EU intervention in the Balkans, East

Timor, South Africa, etc., can provide evidence for those who wish to debate these issues in an informed manner.

The scope for such a debate in the context of Ireland is almost nil. Despite major intervention by the EU, there has been little in the way of reconstruction in the social sense. Demands for a clear commitment to human rights have seen some progress, whether in the establishment of Human Rights Commissions, North and South, the appointment of a Children's Commissioner in Northern Ireland, the robust role played by the Police Ombudsman in Northern Ireland, etc.; but there has been no push from the international community to prioritise the human rights retraining of the judiciary, the establishment of a mechanism to deal formally with past human rights abuses, or the formal incorporation of women into peace negotiations in line with UN Security Council Resolution 1325. A well-established tradition of community development received an initial boost from Peace I, only to experience a reversal of priorities in Peace II. In short, many of the elements of good practice as regards reconstruction globally have been limited or non-existent in the case of Ireland. In many ways, the experience of the decade since the cease-fires has been one of lost opportunity in terms of conflict transformation and reconstruction. We will examine this conclusion further in Chapter 6.

---

[1] Salih, M.A. (1999) 'Post-War Reconstruction in Northern Ethiopia: Relief Society of Tigray and its International NGO Partners', in *Voices From Africa: Conflict, Peace-keeping and Reconstruction*, Geneva: UN Non-Governmental Liaison Service, (no. 8). http://www.unsystem.org/ngls/documents/publications.en/voices.africa/number8/4salih.htm

2   International Crisis Group (2001) 'Afghanistan and Central Asia:
     Priorities for Reconstruction and Development', *Crisisweb*.
     http://www.intl-crisis-group.org/projects/showreport.cfm?reportid=497,
     p. i.
3   DFID (2002) *The Reconstruction of Afghanistan, Background Briefing*,
     p. 3. http://www.dfid.gov.uk/Pubs/files/afghanistan_bb_sept2002.pdf
4   World Bank (1998) *Post-Conflict Reconstruction: The Role of the World
     Bank,* Washington, D.C.: World Bank, p. 32.
5   World Bank (1998) *Conflict Prevention and Post-Conflict
     Reconstruction: Perspectives and Prospects,* Paris: World Bank, p. 8.
     http://wbln0018.worldbank.org/Networks/ESSD/icdb.nsf/D4856F112E8
     05DF4852566C9007C27A6/B86BCB448F0C5E9E85256849007831ED/
     $FILE/ParisReport.pdf
6   World Bank (2003) 'South-Central Africa and Great Lakes: DR Congo
     leading the region's road to peace', *Devnews*, 15 May.
     http://web.worldbank.org/WBSITE/EXTERNAL/NEWS/0,,contentMDK:2
     0111747~menuPK:34457~pagePK:64003015~piPK:64003012~theSite
     PK:4607,00.html
7   World Bank (2003) 'Rebuilding a country from the bare minimum: the
     World Bank's work in Afghanistan', *Devnews*, 12 May.
     http://web.worldbank.org/WBSITE/EXTERNAL/NEWS/0,,contentMDK:2
     0111306~menuPK:34457~pagePK:64003015~piPK:64003012~theSite
     PK:4607,00.html
8   World Bank (2003) 'Alleviating poverty in the midst of conflict: the
     World Bank's work in West Bank and Gaza', *Devnews*, 16 May.
     http://web.worldbank.org/WBSITE/EXTERNAL/NEWS/0,,contentMDK:2
     0112008~menuPK:34457~pagePK:64003015~piPK:64003012~theSite
     PK:4607,00.html
9   Moore, D. (2000) 'Levelling the Playing Fields and Embedding Illusions:
     "Post-Conflict" Discourse and Neo-liberal "Development" in War-torn
     Africa', *Review of African Political Economy*, 83, 11–28.
10   Hamre, J. et al. (2003) *Iraq's post-conflict reconstruction: A field review
     and recommendations*, Iraq Reconstruction Assessment Mission, 27
     June–7 July 2003, Washington, D.C.: Center for Strategic and
     International Studies, p. ii.
     http://wwww.reliefweb.int/w/rwb.nsf/0/ab4dbac657ffa217c1256d67003
     9773c?OpenDocument
11   Cited in Collins, C. (1997) 'Reconstructing the Congo', *Review of
     African Political Economy*, 74, 593.
12   http://web.worldbank.org/WBSITE/EXTERNAL/EXTABOUTUS/0
     ,,pagePK:43912~piPK:36602~theSitePK:29708,00.html
13   'Two U.S. Firms Hit Iraq Jackpot'.
     http://www.cbsnews.com/stories/2003/08/28/iraq/main570624.shtml

14 See for example Shah, A. (2003) 'Structural Adjustment – a Major Cause of Poverty'. http://www.globalissues.org/TradeRelated/SAP.asp

15 Del Castillo, G. (2003) *Economic Reconstruction in Post-Conflict Transitions: Lessons for the Democratic Republic of the Congo (DRC)*, Paris: OECD Development Centre. http://www.oecd.org/dev/technics

16 'Law in Action', BBC Radio 4, 19 November 2004.

17 Mungoven, R. (2003) 'Iraq: Donors must learn from Afghanistan – Human rights a priority for reconstruction', Human Rights Watch Press Release, 20 June. http://hrw.org/press/2003/06/iraq062003.htm

18 Human Rights Watch (2003) 'Letter to G8 leaders before Evian-les-Bains summit', Press Release, 29 May. http://hrw.org/press/2003/05/g8ltr.htm

19 Human Rights Watch (2003) 'Human Rights and Iraq's reconstruction: memorandum to June 24 International Donors Meeting', Press Release, 20 June. http://hrw.org/backgrounder/mena/iraq/iraq-memo062003.htm

20 Oxfam (1997) 'The Importance of Engagement: A Strategy for Reconstruction in the Great Lakes Region', Press Release, 21 October. http://www.africaaction.org.docs97/ox9710.htm

21 Stiefel, M. (1999) *Rebuilding after war: Lessons from WSP*, Geneva: War-torn Societies Project, pp. 3–4. http://wsp.dataweb.ch/wsp_publication/toc-6.htm

22 Hayner, P. (2001) *Unspeakable Truths: Confronting State Terror and Atrocity*, New York: Routledge.

23 *Rwanda: Accountability for War Crimes and Genocide*, Special Report 13 (1994) Washington, D.C.: United States Institute of Peace. http://www.usip.org/pubs/specialreports/early/rwanda1.html

24 Peace Agreement between the Government of Sierra Leone and the Revolutionary United Front of Sierra Leone, 1999, Washington, D.C.: United States Institute of Peace. http://www.usip.org/library/pa/sl/sierra_leone_07071999.html#26

25 *From Madness to Hope: the 12-year war in El Salvador: Report of the Commission on the Truth for El Salvador* (1993) Washington, D.C.: United States Institute of Peace. http://www.usip.org/library/tc/doc/reports/el_salvador/tc_es_03151993 toc.html. See also Hayner, P (2001) op. cit., pp. 38–40.

26 Ignatieff, M. (1996) 'Articles of Faith', *Index on Censorship*, 25 (5) 113.

27 *Report of the Chilean National Commission on Truth and Reconciliation* (1993) Notre Dame: University of Notre Dame Press. http://www.derechoschile.com/english/rettig.htm. See also Hayner, P. (2001) op. cit., pp. 35–38.

28 Oxfam (1997) op. cit.

29 Banfield, B., Haufler, V. and Lilly, D. (2003) *Transnational Corporations in Conflict Prone Zones: Public Policy Responses and a Framework for Action*. London: International Alert. http://www.international-alert.org/pdf/pubbus//TNCslinlconflictlpronelzones.pdf

30 Del Castillo, G. (2003) op. cit., pp. 6–9.

31 Kingma, K. (ed.) (2000) *Demobilization in Sub-Saharan Africa: the Development and Security Impacts*. Houndmills: Macmillan, p. 19.

32 Kingma, K. (2000) 'The Impact of Demobilisation', in Kingma, K. (ed.) (2000) op. cit., p. 231.

33 Bruchhaus, E. and Mehreteab, A. (2000) '"Leaving the Warm House": the Impact of Demobilization in Eritrea', in Kingma, K. (ed.) (2000) op. cit., p. 110.

34 Del Castillo, G. (2003) op. cit., p. 8.

35 Gear, S. (2002) *Wishing Us Away: Challenges Facing Ex-Combatants in the 'New' South Africa*, Cape Town: Centre for the Study of Violence and Reconciliation, Violence and Transition Series, vol. 8. http://www.csvr.org.za/papers/papvtp8a.htm

36 Berdal, M. (1996) *Disarmament and Demobilisation after Civil Wars*, Oxford: Oxford University Press/Institute for Strategic Studies, p. 49.

37 Ibid., p. 50.

38 Kingma, K. (2000) 'The Impact of Demobilisation', in Kingma, K. (ed.) (2000) op. cit., p. 225.

39 Ibid., p. 220. See also Bruchhaus, E. and Mehreteab, A. (2000) op. cit., pp. 95–131, and Ayalew, D. and Dercon, S. (2000) '"From the Gun to the Plough": the Macro- and Micro-Level Impact of Demobilization in Ethiopia', in Kingma, K. (ed.) (2000) op. cit., pp. 132–172.

40 Reiman, C. (2001) *Engendering the Field of Conflict Management: Why Gender Does not Matter: thoughts from a theoretical perspective*, Peace Studies Papers, Working Paper 2, University of Bradford: Department of Peace Studies, p. 38.

41 Farr, V. (2003) 'The importance of a gender perspective to successful disarmament, demobilization and reintegration processes', *Disarmament Forum*, 4, UN Institute for Disarmament, pp. 25–35.

42 Cockburn, C. (1991) 'Gender, Armed Conflict and Political Violence', background paper prepared for the World Bank, Washington D.C., June 10–11, p.17. A later version of this paper can be found in Moser, C. and Clark. F. (eds.) (2001) *Victims, Perpetrators or Actors? Gender, armed conflict and political violence*, London: Zed Books, pp.13–29.

43 Vincent, L. (2001) 'Engendering Peace in Africa: a critical enquiry into some current thinking on the role of African Women in Peace-Building', *Africa Journal in Conflict Resolution*, 1, pp.13–30. http://www.accord.org.za/

44 See UN (2002) *Women, Peace and Security. Study submitted by the Secretary-General Pursuant to Security Council Resolution 1325*, New York: UN for country-specific examples.

45 Kvinna Till Kvinna (2004) *Rethink! A handbook for sustainable peace*, Stockholm: Kvinna Foundation, p. 15. http:www.iktk.se/publikationer/rapporter/pdf/Rethink

46 Plenary speech given by Anne Gahongayire, Secretary-General of the Ministry of Gender and Family Promotion, Republic of Rwanda, Salzburg Seminar, Session 417, 'Strengthening Democracy and Governance: Women and Political Power', April 26–May 3, 2004.

47 Hunt, S. and Ogunsanya, K. (2003) 'Women waging peace – making women visible', *Conflict Trends*, 3, 46.

48 Chinkin, C. (n.d.) *Gender, International Society, Law and Policy*, p. 19. http://www.unu.edu/millenium/chinkin.pdf

49 Quoted in Chinkin, C. (2003) *Peace Agreements as a Means for Promoting Gender Equality and Ensuring Participation of Women*, Ottawa: UN Division for the Advancement of Women, Expert Group Meeting, 10–13 November, p. 8.

50 The UK Government signed the Optional Protocol on 17 December 2004.

51 UN Beijing Platform for Action Strategic Objectives, 1995.

52 United Nations Security Council (2000) *Resolution 1325*, New York: UN, p. 2. http://www.un.org/events/res_1325e.pdf

53 Anderson, S. (1999) 'Women and Reconciliation', in *People Building Peace: 35 Inspiring Stories from Around the World*, Utrecht: European Centre for Conflict Prevention, p. 4. http://www.ifor.org/wpp/womrecon

54 Ibid., p. 31.

55 UNDP (2001) *Gender Approaches in Conflict and Post-Conflict Situations*, p. 13.

56 See Northern Ireland Office (2004) *A Commentary on the Northern Ireland Crime Statistics 2003*, Belfast: NIO.

57 Strickland, R. and Duvvury, N. (2003) *Gender Equity and Peacebuilding: from rhetoric to reality: finding the way*, Washington, D.C.: International Centre for Research on Women, p. 9.

58 Ibid., p. 2. http://www.icrw.org/docs/gender_peace_report_0303

59 Myrttinen, H. (2003) 'Disarming masculinities', *Disarmament Forum*, 4, UN Institute for Disarmament, p. 44.

60 Strickland, R. and Duvvury, N. (2003) op. cit., p. 22.

61 *Human Security Now*: Commission on Human Security, an initiative of the Government of Japan, supported by the UN, co-chairs Sadako Ogata and Amartya Sen, New York, 2003, p. 82. http://www.humansecurity-chs.org

62 Ibid., p.115. See also McKay, S. (n.d.) *Women, Human Security and Peacebuilding*. http://www.gmu.edu/academic/hsp/McKay.htm

63 Chinkin, C. (n.d.) *Gender, International Society, Law and Policy*, p. 21. http://www.unu.edu/millenium/chinkin.pdf

64 Sørenson, B. (1998) *Women and Post-Conflict Reconstruction: Issues and Sources*, War-Torn Societies Project, WSP Occasional Paper No 3, UNRISD.

65 Hill, F. (2003) 'Women's contribution to conflict prevention, early warning and disarmament', *Disarmament Forum*, 4, UN Institute for Disarmament, p. 21, making reference to the Women's International League for Peace and Freedom's Women's Budget Project. http://www.unidir.org/gender/

66 Pankhurst, D. (2000) *Women, Gender and Peacebuilding*, Working Paper No.5, University of Bradford, Department of Peace Studies.

67 Strickland, R. and Duvvury, N. (2003) op. cit., p. 12.

68 Ibid., p. 13.

69 Ibid., p. 13.

70 Women's Commission for Refugee Women and Children (2000) *Untapped Potential: Adolescents affected by armed conflict – a review of programs and policies*, New York: Women's Commission for Refugee Women and Children. http://www.womenscommission.org/pdf/adol2.pdf p. 3.

71 Ibid., p. 1.

72 Ibid., p. 9.

73 Arvantakis, J. (2003) *Highly Affected, Rarely Considered: The International Youth Parliament Commission's Report on the Impacts of Globalisation on Young People*, Sydney: International Youth Parliament/Oxfam. http://www.iyp.oxfam.org/campaign/documents/youth_commission_re port/Highly_Affected_Rarely_Considered.pdf p. 114.

74 Machel, G. (1996) *Impact of Armed Conflict on Children*, New York: Unicef. http://www.unicef.org/graca/a51-306_en.pdf

75 Women's Commission for Refugee Women and Children (2002) *Precious resources: Adolescents in the reconstruction of Sierra Leone*, New York: Women's Commission for Refugee Women and Children, p. 3. http://www.reliefweb.int/w/rwb.nsf/0/1c2201b2a0ae673849256c6a000 9c5cc?OpenDocument

76 Goodhand, J. with Atkinson, P. (2001) *Conflict and Aid: enhancing the Peacebuilding Impact of International Engagement. A Synthesis of Findings from Afghanistan, Liberia and Sri Lanka*, London: International Alert, p. 19.

77 See 'Pentagon forced to withdraw leaflet linking aid to information on Taliban', *The Guardian*, 6 May 2004.

78 Goodhand, J. with Atkinson, P. (2001) op. cit., p. 24.

79 Ibid., p. 33.

80 Ibid., p. 36.

81 Ibid., p. 37.

82 Ibid., p. 38.

83 World Bank (2003) 'Nation-building and reconstruction: the World Bank's work in Timor-Leste', *Devnews*, 13 May. http://web.worldbank.org/WBSITE/EXTERNAL/NEWS/0,,contentMDK:2 0111418~menuPK:34457~pagePK:64003015~piPK:64003012~theSite PK:4607,00.html

84 World Bank (1998) *Post-Conflict Reconstruction: The Role of the World Bank*, op. cit., p. v.

85 Shonali, S. and Wam, Per. (2002) *The Conflict Analysis Framework (CAF): Identifying conflict-related obstacles to development*, Washington, D.C.: World Bank, Conflict prevention and reconstruction unit, Social Development Department, Dissemination Note No. 5. http://wbln0018.worldbank.org/Networks/ESSD/icdb.nsf/D4856F112E8 05DF4852566C9007C27A6/2EC2E7EBA4A2885485256CE9006795A5/ $FILE/CPR+5+final+legal.pdf

86 Ibid.

87 World Bank (1998) *Post-Conflict Reconstruction: The Role of the World Bank*, op. cit., p. 1.

88 Ibid., p. 47.

89 Leonhardt, M. (2000) *Conflict Impact Assessment of EU Development Co-operation with ACP Countries: a Review of Literature and Practice*, London: International Alert and Saferworld, p. 5. http://www.international-alert.org/pdf/pubdev/conflict%20impact%20 pcia.pdf

90 G8 (2001) Miyazaki Initiatives for Conflict Resolution, p. 1. http://www.mofa.go.jp/policy/economy/summit/2000/pdfs/initiative.pdf

91 Ibid., p. 31.

92 Orjuela, C. (2003) 'Building Peace in Sri Lanka: A Role for Civil Society?' *Journal of Peace Research* 40 (2), 195–212.

93 Gellner, E. (1994) *Conditions of Liberty: Civil Society and Its Rivals*, Harmondsworth: Penguin, p. 168.

94 Putnam, R. (1992) *Making Democracy Work: Civil Traditions in Modern Italy*, Princeton: Princeton University Press, p. 167. See also Coleman, J. (1990) *Foundations of Social Theory*, Cambridge, Massachusetts: Harvard University Press.

95 Belloni, R. (2001) 'Civil Society and Peacebuilding in Bosnia and Herzogovina', *Journal of Peace Research* 38 (2), 166–167.

96 Ibid., p. 176.
97 Ibid., p. 177.
98 Ibid., p. 175.
99 Moore, D. (2000) 'Levelling the Playing Fields and Embedding Illusions: "Post-Conflict" Discourse and Neo-liberal "Development" in War-torn Africa', *Review of African Political Economy*, 83, 15.
100 Ibid., pp. 21–22.
101 Ibid., p. 22.
102 Ibid., p. 24. Quotation from World Bank: World Bank (1998) *Post-Conflict Reconstruction: The Role of the World Bank*, op. cit., p. 17.
103 Stiefel, M. (1999) *Rebuilding after war: Lessons from WSP*, Geneva: War-torn Societies Project, p. 10.
    http://wsp.dataweb.ch/wsp_publication/toc-6.htm
104 See European Agency for Reconstruction website for News, July 2003.
    http://www.ear.eu.int/publications/news-a1g2p3.htm
105 European Parliament, Motion for a Resolution on the situation in Afghanistan one year after the signing of the Bonn Agreement, 9 January 2003.
    http://www.europarl.eu.int/meetdocs/committees/libe/20031103/p5_b(2003)0026_en.pdf

Chapter 4

Poverty, Inequality and Conflict in Ireland

Introduction

The previous chapters have explored various aspects of poverty, inequality and conflict internationally. This chapter examines the three concepts in relation to Ireland. We begin the analysis with the ways poverty has been defined in Ireland, both North and South, and provide an overview of its nature and extent in the respective jurisdictions. As explained in Chapter 2, there is an expanding international debate over whether the focus should be on 'poverty' or more broadly on 'inequality'. Inequality, of course, is not only about social justice but also about the adverse and costly consequences of an unequal society. There is now a growing volume of empirical evidence which suggests that extensive inequality leads to higher levels of ill-health, greater mortality differentials, high levels of crime and violent death and generally more unstable social order. In the second section we consider the nature and extent of inequality in Ireland, and in the third section we focus upon the social, economic and financial impact of the conflict, particularly in respect to Northern Ireland.

Poverty

The principal problem is how to measure the extent of poverty, assuming that an agreed definition of poverty can be arrived at. The UK government does not define the term while the Irish government uses the following definition:

> People are living in poverty if their income and resources (material, cultural and social) are so inadequate as to preclude them from having a standard of living which is regarded as acceptable by Irish society generally. As a result of inadequate income and resources people may be excluded and marginalised from participating in activities which are considered the norm for other people in society.[1]

For its understanding of poverty, the UK government publishes two sets of poverty related statistics. The first is based on the Family Resources Survey (FRS) and records the numbers of people living in Households Below Average Income (HBAI). Figures are provided for the number of children and the number of adults living below various thresholds, and are presented by region (with the exception of Northern Ireland). The second set is published in an annual report called *Opportunity for All* and monitors deprivation on three dimensions: poverty and low income, stage in the family life cycle and 'communities' or localities. More recently, the government has suggested a 'tiered' approach for measuring child poverty which would combine income and deprivation measures.[2] The two sets of statistics relate to Britain and are not broken down for Northern Ireland.

The Programme for Government for Northern Ireland includes a commitment to deal with poverty:

We recognise the inequalities in the life experiences of our citizens in terms of poverty, health, housing, education and economic opportunity and disability and we are determined to tackle them.[3]

Yet up to the time of the suspension of the Executive in October 2002, it had produced no agreed definition or measure of poverty. There are, however, a considerable number of indicators, similar to those published annually in *Opportunity for All,* which have been collected by the Northern Ireland Statistical and Research Agency (NISRA). In addition, a new index of area deprivation based on administrative data has been developed by a team from Oxford University and is now known as the Noble Index.[4] This is based on seven domains: low income, employability and unemployment, health and well-being, education, access to services, social environment, and housing, with a number of indicators pertinent to each domain.

In 2002, OFM/DFM commissioned a large research project – the Poverty and Social Exclusion Northern Ireland study (PSENI).[5] Its principal objective was to define and measure the nature and extent of poverty. Drawing on the British Millennium study carried out in 1999 by a team of researchers from Bristol, Loughborough and York Universities[6] and work carried out by the Ministry of Development in New Zealand, the study constructed a consensual definition of poverty. First, a sample of the general public was asked to decide on what they considered were the basic necessities of life. A second sample was then asked if they possessed items that 50 per cent of the population considered necessities. If they did not, they were asked if this was because they did not want it or because they could not afford it. Households were then defined as poor if they could not afford three or more selected items.

Using this measure, some 185,500 households, or 29.6 per cent of all households in Northern Ireland were poor in 2002/2003. In total, some half a million people were living in poverty and of these 148,900 were children. Interestingly, the relative income measure of 70 per cent of the median income before housing costs, produced a similar proportion of households living in poverty. The figure dropped to 23 per cent when measured at 60 percent of the median income before housing costs (see Figure 4.1). Similar figures were found in the Northern Ireland Household Panel survey[7] carried out a year earlier, where at 70 per cent of the median before housing costs, the proportion in poverty was 28 per cent and at 60 per cent of the median, 21 per cent.[8]

Figure 4.1 Proportion of persons below median income thresholds, Ireland, North and South

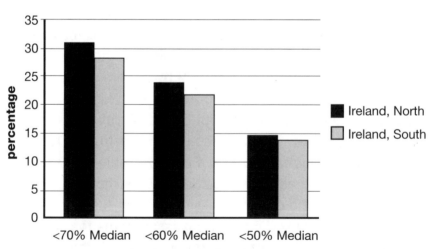

Source: Hillyard et al. (2003) *Bare Necessities: Poverty and Social Exclusion in Northern Ireland – key findings*, Belfast: Democratic Dialogue. p. 38.

Information on poverty in the South is provided by the Economic and Social Research Institute and drawn from the longitudinal Living in Ireland Survey (1994–2001). Two different measures of poverty are used: 'at risk of poverty' and 'consistent poverty'. 'At risk of poverty' is a measure of relative income poverty, using various proportions of household income (40 to 70 per cent). 'Consistent poverty' combines risk of poverty with lack of at least one of eight basic items such as adequate clothing. Both measures are based on equivalised income[9] and use mean and median figures. As a direct result of sustained economic growth over the last decade, the level of consistent poverty had fallen steadily from 15.1 per cent in 1994 to 5.2 per cent in 2001. When measured by 60 per cent of the median income, some 21.1 per cent of the population were in poverty compared with 15.6 per cent in 1994.[10]

The PSENI study allows comparisons to be made between Ireland North and South using the same definitions of poverty and the same methods of equivalisation. Using the 'consistent poverty' measure, some 6.9 per cent of households in Northern Ireland are poor compared with 5.2 per cent in the South (see Figure 4.2).

Using 'relative poverty', the rates are considerably higher in both Northern Ireland and the South. For example, at the below 70 per cent median threshold, some 30.6 per cent of persons are in poor households in Northern Ireland compared with 28.2 per cent in the South. This 'overall poverty' rate for Northern Ireland is very close to that obtained using a 'consensual definition' of poverty (PSENI) – 29.6 per cent compared with 30.6 per cent – and suggests that the 'relative poverty' rate is a much more realistic measurement of the extent of poverty than the 'consistent measure'.

Figure 4.2 Households in consistent poverty, Ireland, North and South compared

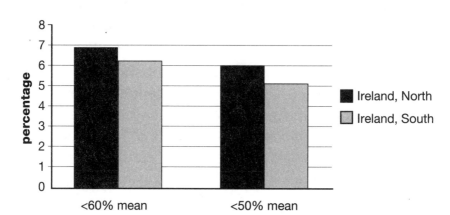

Source: Hillyard et al. (2003) *Bare Necessities: Poverty and Social Exclusion in Northern Ireland – key findings,* Belfast: Democratic Dialogue, p. 37.

There is now a considerable amount of empirical evidence available in Ireland, North and South, on which types of households and persons are most likely to be living in poverty. The PSENI study found that the risk of poverty varied greatly with different socio-economic profiles. For example, 36 per cent of Catholic households were living in poverty compared with 25 per cent of Protestant households. Lone parents experienced considerable risk of poverty with some 67 per cent living in poor households. Other high risk groups included the disabled, the unemployed, and the long-term sick, the latter having a poverty risk of 42 per cent.

In a report commissioned by OFM/DFM, which was part of the research and evaluation strategy for the Government's *New Targeting Social Need*, the possibility of establishing a baseline of poverty from existing government data sources was examined.[11] It analysed the bottom 30 per cent of the income distribution, since the bottom three deciles are likely to encompass individuals in households below half of the mean. Using Continuous Household Survey (CHS) data it considered key aspects of the socio-economic profiles of all individuals, children, working-age adults and pensioners. It was able to identify the extent to which certain groups are more or less likely to be found in the bottom 30 per cent. Lone parents again exhibit a high risk along with households in which one or more adults are unemployed.

As shown above, the general risk of poverty is very similar North and South, and while no detailed comparison of risk groups has been carried out using the same poverty measures, certain trends are clear. In Northern Ireland, households in which someone has a disability have a poverty risk of more than 50 per cent. A similar figure is recorded in the South where the household reference person has a disability. Households where the reference person was retired had a one in three risk of living in relative poverty in the South. The equivalent risk in Northern Ireland was slightly greater than one in four.[12]

In Ireland, North and South, very similar proportions of children are growing up in households with below average household income. In the South 23 per cent of children live in households with less than 60 per cent of the median income while at the 70 per cent median income line the risk is 31 per cent. The poverty risk for children in Northern Ireland is slightly greater than in the South on both measures – 27 per cent and 34 per cent, respectively. The same is the case for lone parents.

The border area has been shown to be particularly deprived. A study based on 1991 census data by geographers at

Queen's University, the University of Ulster and NUI Maynooth, found that in both jurisdictions the border region was more deprived than the rest of the island.[13] In addition, while the patterns of unemployment were similar on the northern and southern sides of the border, economic dependency was higher south of the border together with a higher proportion of households lacking basic amenities such as baths, showers and central heating. Overall, this area is characterised by lower than average labour market participation rates – the clearest indicator of economic malaise and high poverty. For men, the 1991 censuses showed that border participation rates were about the same for Northern Ireland (72.1 per cent) and the South (72.9 per cent) compared to overall rates of 72.7 (North) and 74.0 (South). For women, however, there was a marked difference either side of the border with a rate of 42.2 per cent for Northern Ireland and only 28.5 per cent for the South, which corresponded to the gender difference between Northern Ireland and South as a whole.

This changed during the 1990s. In the South the expansion of employment 'created a new set of jobs for a new set of workers'.[14] Women benefited more than men in the sense that they were drawn into the labour market from 'inactivity'. While unemployment fell for both men and women in the South from 1993 onwards, 'inactivity' rates for men remained at high levels, falling slightly at the end of the decade. So the change principally benefited unemployed rather than 'inactive' men. For women, declining unemployment was matched by a steady decline in inactivity rates. The effect was a convergence in unemployment and inactivity between North and South, a convergence that has been reinforced by rising non-employment amongst women in Northern Ireland between 1995 and 2000.

Labour Force surveys carried out North and South allow comparisons to be made for NUTS3 areas, of which there are five for Northern Ireland and eight for the South. 'Border' is one of the Southern NUTS3 areas and it covers the entire length of the border in a somewhat undifferentiated manner. In 2001, Border had the highest ILO-unemployment rate of any NUTS3 area in Ireland, North or South (See Figure 4.3). High unemployment tends to be strongly associated with low participation rates. Border has the second lowest participation rate in Ireland; the worst rate belongs to Belfast, which also has the fourth highest unemployment rate. The 'West and South of Northern Ireland' area is a close fifth in terms of unemployment but has a mid-range participation rate.[15] Whatever might be claimed about the economic benefits of peace, there has been no real transformation of the economies of these areas.

Within the Northern border area there are stark differences in unemployment rates at local level. In Armagh district council area in 1991, Callan Bridge ward had the highest unemployment rate (41 per cent) and Rich Hill the lowest (5 per cent).[16] By 2001, the Callan Bridge rate had come down to 17.6 per cent and Rich Hill to 3.2 per cent.[17] In Fermanagh, Rosslea had the highest unemployment rate (34 per cent), while Ballinamallard had the lowest at 11 per cent (1991). Rosslea's rate was down to 13.3 per cent in 2001 and Ballinamallard's dropped to 4.6 per cent. Rich Hill has a 95.6 per cent non-Catholic population (2001). Ballinamallard is 81.7 per cent non-Catholic. In contrast, the high unemployment areas are overwhelmingly Catholic – Callan Bridge, 90 per cent, and Rosslea, 85 per cent. This reflects the pattern for Northern Ireland as a whole for 2001 where 'there is still a positive relationship between the percentage of

Figure 4.3 ILO unemployment and participation rates, NUTS3 regions

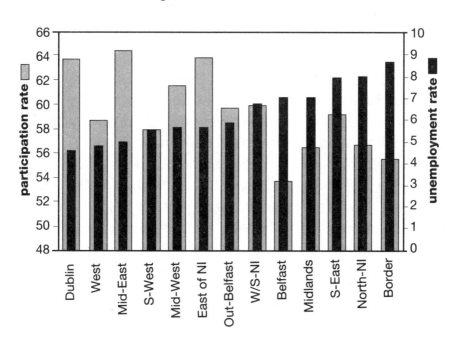

Source: Northern Ireland Labour Force Surveys and the Quarterly National Household Surveys.

a ward's residents with a Catholic community background and the ward's unemployment rate'.[18]

Inequality

The spectacular development of the Irish economy over the last 14 years has been accompanied by growing inequalities. In the 2003 *Human Development Report*, which was launched in Dublin and ranked countries on a range of social and economic statistics, Ireland was ranked twelfth overall and came third in terms of GNP per capita. But on a range of measures it lagged behind a list of countries. From 1987 to

2000 the ratio of disposable income received by the top quintile to that of the bottom quintile rose from 6.8 to 8.38.[19] In an analysis of the last seven budgets the CORI Justice Commission has shown how there has been a dramatic widening of the rich/poor gap as more was distributed to those who were better off than those who were the poorest in Irish society. For example, a person with an income of over €50,000 was €17,224 a year better off in 2004 than they were in 1997, compared with a single unemployed person who was €2,613 better off as a result of tax and welfare changes and wage growth.[20] In 1997 the average pay of chief executives in the top quartile was some 23 times the wage of a typical production worker. These trends, which suggest a widening of the gap between rich and poor, however, are not reflected in the most widely used measure of the extent of inequality, the Gini coefficient. This has declined from 33 per cent in 1997 to 29 per cent in 2001.[21] It is difficult to interpret these contradictory trends. However, a Gini coefficient of 29 per cent is relatively high compared with Germany, which has a Gini coefficient of 22 per cent. One of the starkest facts is the level of illiteracy. At the start of the twentieth century, it was estimated that about 12 per cent of the population in Ireland were illiterate. Now, at the beginning of the 21st century, an OECD study of adult literacy found that 23 per cent of those tested did not have the literacy skills necessary to function in contemporary society.[22]

A study by Amárach Consulting, which explored the views of 1,000 people on the quality of life in Ireland, found that some 77 per cent said that their quality of life had improved. However, some 10 per cent – mainly the elderly and lower social classes – said that it had not. The explanation given lay in the growing income inequality.[23]

The main source for ascertaining income inequality in Northern Ireland has been the Family Expenditure Survey (FES). The survey began in 1968 but no calculations were made of income inequality using the Gini coefficient until 1998/1999. Based on average gross weekly household income, it stood at 39 per cent in 1998/99. By 2001/2002 the figure had dropped by 10 percentage points to 29 per cent.[24] The reasons for this large decline are difficult to ascertain. The increase in the number of jobs and the introduction of the minimum wage may have had an impact. A Gini coefficient was calculated based on the PSENI data for 2002/03 and was found to be 42 per cent, which is considerably higher than the figure from the FES data. The PSENI data also showed that the top four deciles income groups in Northern Ireland possessed 67 per cent of the income.[25]

Recently, the Institute for Fiscal Studies published a detailed analysis of trends in income and expenditure inequality in Britain. It is highly likely that Northern Ireland has experienced similar trends.[26] Figure 4.4 shows the growth in inequality as measured by the Gini coefficient between 1974 and 2002. It fluctuated up and down during the 1960s, declined over much of the 1970s when Labour governments pursued redistributive policies, then increased rapidly from 1979 when the Conservative government was returned to power under Mrs Thatcher and has remained high with only a slight downturn since New Labour came to power in 1997.

Earnings Surveys, which are carried out on an annual basis, provide further information on the income divide within Northern Ireland.[27] The 2003 Survey shows that 80 per cent of full-time employees earned less than £28,550 per year, while 20 per cent earned less than £12,275. Some 10 per

Figure 4.4 Income Gini coefficient for Great Britain, 1974–2002

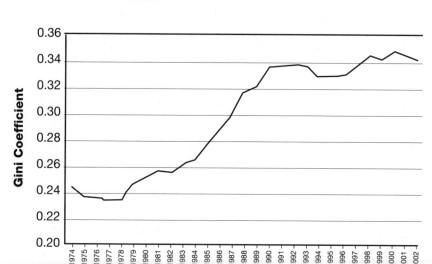

Reproduced with kind permission from Goodman, A. and Oldfield, Z. (2004) *Permanent Differences? Income and Expenditure Inequality in the 1990s and 2002*, London: Institute of Fiscal Studies. p. 10.

cent of full-time employees earned more than £34,400 per year and 2 per cent more than £53,000.[28] The gap between the top 10 per cent of earners and the bottom 10 per cent widened for both males and females over the year. Between 2002 and 2003, earnings of the top 10 per cent of men increased by 3.7 per cent and the bottom 10 per cent increased by 2.6 per cent. The top 10 per cent of women saw an increase of 2.2 per cent and the bottom 10 per cent an increase of 5.1 per cent.[29]

The inequalities in health on the island of Ireland have been extensively documented.[30] In Ireland (South), between 1989 and 1998 the death rates for all causes of death were three times higher in the lowest occupational class than in the highest. In relation to cancer, the death rates for all types were twice as high among the lowest occupational classes as for the highest classes. For strokes, it is nearly three times higher and six times higher for accidents. For suicide, the incidence of male suicide is far higher in the lower socio-economic groups as compared with the highest groups. Some groups face extreme health inequalities. For example, members of the Traveller community will live between 10 and 12 years less than the population as a whole.[31]

In Northern Ireland the gap in health status between the rich and the poor has been widening over the past few decades. People who live in affluent areas can expect to live longer than those who live in the most deprived areas, and infant deaths rates are 50 per cent higher in the most deprived areas compared with the most affluent.[32] An analysis of mortality rates for the whole of the UK between 1991 and 1993 shows that there is a clear socio-economic gradient in mortality for all the countries of the UK, with the highest rates in Social Class V. However, the relative difference between social classes did vary between regions and there were particularly wide variations in Northern Ireland (see Table 4.1). For example, deaths from all causes were five times higher in Social Class V compared with Social Class I, and deaths from accidents were seven times higher.[33]

In a recent secondary analysis of the Health and Wellbeing Surveys in Northern Ireland it was found that while only 10.5 per cent of respondents in professional/managerial positions reported that their general health was not good, the figure for unskilled respondents was nearly two and half times as great. Health was also positively related to affluence.[34] The most important finding from the study was that:

Table 4.1 Difference in death rates for men aged 20–64 between Social Class I and Social Class V in Northern Ireland, 1991 to 1993

Category	Differential
All causes	5x
Ischaemic heart disease	4x
Stroke	10.6x
All cancers	4x
Lung cancer	6x
Accidents	7x
Suicide	7x

Source: Uren, Z. et al. (2001) 'Geographic variation in mortality by Social Class and alternative social classifications', in C. Griffiths and J. Fitzpatrick (eds.) *Geographic Variations in Health*, London: Stationery Office, pp. 342–355.

Whilst the majority of Section 75 indicators had no significant impact on the general health of respondents, in turn the three most significant factors that did – respondent's age, social class and their relative affluence – do not feature as factors of inequality in Section 75 at all.[35]

The Convention on the Elimination of All Forms of Discrimination Against Women (CEDAW) Shadow Report on Ireland 2004 noted how class and gender were linked in relation to health. It concluded that, 'Within the area of health many inequalities in the system persist, and many marginalised women experience particular difficulties in accessing services.'[36]

There are wide inequalities in education in Northern Ireland. While the proportion of people aged 16–24 without a basic qualification has fallen from 38.9 per cent in 1992 to 30 per cent in 2001, the proportion of school leavers achieving no qualifications rose from 2.7 per cent in 1998/99 to 5.2 per cent in 2001/02.[37] The 11-plus examination, on which selection to grammar schools is based, is a major barrier for many working-class children. For example, in 2002 less than 2 per cent of the children from the Shankill area of Belfast sat the exam.[38]

There are also inequalities in the current system of local taxation. Based on the rateable value of property, the rate burden has become increasingly regressive in the absence of any revaluation since 1973. Thus, in 2001/02 a household with a weekly household income of less than £101 per week paid 11.6 per cent of their income in rates compared with 2.5 per cent of a household earning more than £401.[39] It is planned that a less regressive system based on capital value will be introduced in 2007.

There is a growing problem of homelessness in Northern Ireland. In 2002/2003, 17,150 households presented themselves as homeless – a rise of 4.4 per cent on the previous year.[40] In the same period it was estimated that some 45,000 households – 6.5 per cent of all households – possessed a second home.[41]

In a number of areas the middle classes in Northern Ireland have fared well despite the conflict. They have benefited from the high rates of public expenditure and the associated large number of public sector jobs. Civil servants, teachers and other professional public sector workers have had salaries on a par with those in Great Britain while wages of manual workers working in the private sector have remained consistently lower than their counterparts in Great Britain.

Over the years the middle classes have paid significantly lower property rates than middle class households in the rest of the UK. In addition, there have been no separate water and sewerage charges. Perhaps most important, the policy of selection at 11-plus, coupled with a well-endowed grammar school system supported by state funds, has provided a high quality education system for children of the middle classes. Finally, as housing costs in Northern Ireland have been consistently lower than in many other parts of the UK, the disposable income of the middle classes in Northern Ireland will have been greater.

New car registration of luxury cars provides one indicator of the amount of disposable income in a region. Unfortunately, the published statistics do not break down registrations by make and model although this information is recorded electronically and could be made available at little expense. As a result it is impossible to make precise comparisons. However, based on a selection of the makes, which cater mainly for the upper end of the market – such as Alpha Romeos, BMWs, Ferraris, Jaguars and Porsches – it is possible to produce comparative figures for total registrations of these makes per 100,000 of the population for the regions. On this indicator, Northern Ireland ranks third in the UK, with only the South East and the West Midlands registering a higher proportion of the more expensive makes of car.[42]

Inequalities also impact on social cohesion: a growing volume of evidence suggests that societies that are more equal also are more socially cohesive, while societies that are more unequal have greater differences in life expectancy and ill-health.[43] Inequality not only impacts on health, it leads to higher rates of crime, violence, homicide, alcohol-abuse and even car accidents. Much of the evidence has been brought together by Richard Wilkinson in a book entitled *Unhealthy Societies: The Afflictions of Inequality*.[44] For example, drawing on the work of Kaplan in the US, he shows that differences in income inequality may account for as much as half of the very large differences in homicide rates in the US. Similarly, recent work by Dorling analysing the 13,000 murders in England and Wales between January 1981 and December 2000, shows that the increase in murder which has taken place over the period has been concentrated almost exclusively in men of working age living in the poorest parts of the country.[45]

There is, however, debate about how to explain the relationships. Wilkinson argues that the association between income inequality and other social phenomena (particularly health) can be explained by psychosocial factors. Perceptions of place in the social hierarchy produce negative emotions, which have real impacts on the body through stress and other mechanisms. At the same time, these factors affect external behaviour fostering a lack of trust and a whole raft of anti-social behaviour. Other researchers place more emphasis on the role of material factors.[46] They emphasise the effects of income inequality, lack of individual resources and the systematic lack of investment in people, health, education, and physical and social infrastructure.

In relation to Northern Ireland, there has been no research that specifically considers the impact, if any, that high levels of poverty and inequality have had on the conflict. At a macro level it could be argued that there appears to be little or no impact. The conflict began during a period of relatively low inequality and some of the most intense conflict occurred in the early and late 1970s when the levels of inequality were declining. Peace came when the levels of inequality were the highest. It would, however, be naïve to argue at this level of generality. It is widely accepted, for example, that the perceived differences in the allocation of public resources between Protestants and Catholics were central to the development of the civil rights movement.[47] It is therefore logical to argue that the growing inequalities could have a similar impact on different groups and different strata in society and lead to new forms of conflict. There needs, therefore, to be a more nuanced approach to the analysis which would attempt to explore the impact that inequality has on people's lives both in the material and psychological sense.

The impact of the conflict

In Chapter 1 we presented figures on the number of people killed and injured in the conflict. The harm, however, goes much further, and relatively little research has been carried out to measure the financial, psychological, social and economic costs of the conflict over 30 years.

Impacts on health and social well-being

The impact of the conflict on people's health has been recently reviewed in a Health, Social Services and Public Safety publication.[48] A number of studies by Cairns and Wilson found a link between the level of political violence in different areas and psychological well-being.[49] *The Cost of the Troubles Study* conducted in 1999 also found that there was a significant difference between those reporting poor health in areas that had experienced intense violence and those reporting poor health in low intensity areas.[50] The extent to which the differences in poor health were due to the conflict or to deprivation is, however, unclear. A more robust analysis of the relationship between the troubles and health has been carried out recently based on a secondary analysis of the Health and Wellbeing Surveys of 1997 and 2001. These surveys included a number of questions relating to conflict. Although they were based on the respondents' perceptions, nevertheless they showed that these perceptions may have a substantial impact on the general and mental health of the respondents.[51] People were asked about the level of violence in their area since 1969, the impact that it has had on their own lives and that of their family and the extent to which they worried about the political situation in Northern Ireland. Respondents who said that they experienced 'not very much' violence in their neighbourhood were more likely to report good general health and had a better GHQ score.[52] Those who said that they were affected 'a lot' or 'quite a lot' by the conflict-related events were also significantly more likely to report poor mental health.[53]

More recently, the Northern Ireland Association for Mental Health has revealed that the prevalence of mental health problems in Northern Ireland is 25 per cent higher than in England, while the money spent for the care of people with such problems is 25 per cent less. They concluded that the reason for the higher prevalence can be put down to two interconnected factors: 'socio-economic deprivation' and 'the legacy of the troubles', though how they are connected is not teased out.[54]

The conflict and its continuing effects may be responsible for high tranquilliser usage. A recent survey showed that while the lifetime prevalence figures for illegal drug intake are very similar across Ireland, North and South, a significant disparity exists in the case of prescribed sedatives, tranquillisers and anti-depressants use. The Northern Ireland figure for people who have ever used these drugs was 22 per cent, almost double that for the rest of Ireland (12 per cent). The lifetime prevalence rate for the 55–64 age group in Northern Ireland was 30 per cent. For all age groups, the female rate (28.5 per cent) was almost twice the male rate.[55] The volume of prescribed anti-depressants in Northern Ireland nearly doubled (×1.8) between 1989 and 1993. But from 1993 to the end of the decade prescriptions rose by more than 300 per cent.[56] In 2002, one clinical psychologist claimed: 'What we are seeing now is that people still do not feel safe. We may have a political peace process but on the ground there is still a war psychology. People live in fear of their lives.'[57]

There is growing concern about suicide, especially the rising rates of suicide among men throughout Ireland.[58] In Northern Ireland the overall suicide rate for men has risen by 31 per cent over the last ten years. This compares to a rise of less than 5 per cent for Ireland (South) and a drop of 11 per cent across England and Wales. There is a particular focus on younger age groups, where up to a third of all deaths are accounted for by suicide.[59] In Northern Ireland, the suicide rate for men in the 25–34 age group increased by an astonishing 105 per cent between 1992 and 2002, standing at 2.4 times the overall male rate. This age group now accounts for over a third of all male suicides.

Some groups have raised specific concerns about ill-health and premature deaths, possibly caused by CR and CS gases, and by the non-ionising radiation emitted by widely used surveillance and communications equipment.[60]

Two of the main factors behind persistently high mortality and morbidity in post-conflict situations identified in Chapter 2 –

technical regress and budget reduction – would not seem to be obvious factors in Northern Ireland. Arguably, the introduction of Direct Rule from Westminster in the early 1970s led to *increases* in social expenditures, including spending on health services, above the levels that would otherwise have been expected. In this sense, 'grievance' played a part in stimulating better health provision. By the end of the 1990s infant mortality rates, for example, were down from very high pre-conflict rates to below those of Scotland, Wales, England and Ireland (South).[61] On the other hand, death rates from cancer have been higher in Northern Ireland than in the South (by about 10 per cent) since the mid-1970s.

The 'technical regress' – the worsening of conditions for maintaining good health – was unquestionably a factor in neighbourhoods most affected by violence of one type or another. There were periods when daily life became very difficult. Public service provision of all kinds was interrupted periodically, and severely, during the early years of the conflict. Private services were similarly affected and more prone to capital flight. The long-term and chronic underinvestment in public transport was one of the more important factors affecting daily life and employment opportunities in the poorest areas.[62] Significantly, there is evidence of exclusion from public and private services in the case of hospitals with accident and emergency provision, doctors, evening classes, public transport, pay phones, petrol stations, corner shops and banks.[63]

Social impacts

The social costs of the troubles have been considerable. Intimidation, displacement and migration have occurred on a

massive scale, leading to increased social segregation.
Migration is typically a major feature of any conflict. Yet
conflict-related migration is not a well-researched area in the
case of Northern Ireland.[64] The most quoted figure concerns
internally displaced persons in the 1969–1972 period, during
which an estimated 60,000 people were forced out of their
homes, many of whom crowded into West Belfast.[65] There
are no readily available statistics on the numbers of people
who have moved from Northern Ireland to the South or
Britain, and no developed method for distinguishing 'social'
and 'economic' migrants from conflict 'refugees'. The most
recent estimate of the prevalence of displacement within
Northern Ireland suggests that 54,000 households have been
forced to move because of attack, intimidation or
harassment.[66]

In May 2000 the Northern Ireland Affairs Committee decided
to examine:

> the incidence in Northern Ireland of the practice of
> paramilitary organisations of intimidating residents into
> relocating within, or leaving, the Province, and the
> alleged causes; the steps being taken by Government
> and law enforcement agencies to eliminate this activity;
> the response of the Government and public bodies to
> persons claiming to have been forced from their homes
> through paramilitary intimidation; and the assistance
> available to persons affected by such intimidation who
> subsequently reside, permanently or temporarily, in Great
> Britain.[67]

The inquiry established that no reliable information existed
on all the types of enforced movement to destinations
within and outside of Northern Ireland and concluded that

'there needs to be a significantly more accurate definition of the extent of the problem, and the pattern of relocation'.

Police Service for Northern Ireland (PSNI) evidence to the inquiry distinguished six types of 'paramilitary intimidation': sectarian intimidation, victims of paramilitary feuds, alleged criminals, disputes with paramilitaries, victims of racial intimidation and members of the security forces/prison officers/public officials.

The Northern Ireland Housing Executive administers a Special Purchase of Evacuated Dwelling (SPED) scheme under which the homes of those certified by the Chief Constable as under threat can be purchased. The SPED scheme is open to all owner occupiers but, according to PSNI, the pattern of threats has been such that about 40 per cent of applications come from police officers.[68] This rehousing scheme for owner occupiers cost £33 million in 2002–2003.[69]

The Northern Ireland Affairs Committee inquiry found that some types of enforced migration had increased since the mid-1990s. A subsequent study of 'exiles' to Britain suggests that 'expulsions' (people forced to leave under threat from armed groups) are currently running at four individuals a month, although since 1994 there was 'an increasing tendency to expel whole families rather than individuals'.[70]

Clearly, the experience of refugees and those internally displaced ranges from a well-compensated state-supported move to one in which most, if not all, assets and employment are lost.

One consequence of intimidation and enforced migration is greater residential segregation. This in turn may reinforce conflict between 'interface areas' which has been a notable feature of the post-1994 period. In Belfast, 98 per cent of social housing estates are 'segregated' in the sense of consisting mainly of Catholics or Protestants.[71] The most segregated places are also the poorest areas.

Interface conflict has worsened over the last ten years. As Jarman observes:

> the hardening of territorial boundaries and conflict between communities has further increased the scale and the depth of segregation between the two major communities. Many nationalists and unionists live ever more segregated and separated lives. Residential areas, social environments, sporting and cultural activities, education and worship are all primarily carried on among and within one's own community.[72]

The policy response to segregation has largely been a pragmatic one of building new barriers, walls and fences between communities, or reinforcing and raising old ones.[73] Seven of Belfast's 17 segregation barriers have been built since 1993. The total cost of this investment in division has not been made public but runs into tens of millions of pounds. The cost of policing the Holy Cross dispute in 2001–2002 was sufficient to employ 40 people on average wages for a year.[74]

The challenges of political and social conflict for future generations are starkly illustrated in Connolly's work on political and cultural awareness among 3–6 year olds:

> Half of all three years olds are able to demonstrate some awareness of the cultural/political significance of at least one event or symbol. This rose to 90 per cent of six year olds.[75]

While the recognition of difference does not necessarily translate into sectarianism, by the age of six, about 15 per cent of children are making sectarian statements. Residential segregation and segregated/denominational schooling are the main factors implicated in the production and reinforcement of such prejudices.[76]

Economic impacts

Just as residential areas have been a key site of the conflict, workplaces have likewise reflected political and social divisions. Exclusion from employment was central among the grievances of the 1960s in the build up to armed conflict, and 'fair employment' remained one of the most active areas of politics and policy for the duration of the conflict.[77] Catholic labour market exclusion, especially of men, became the touchstone of the equality debate and continues to be vigorously contested.[78]

Most of the policy development of the last 30 years focused on employer discrimination. This was understandable given the degree of institutionalised and politicised hostility towards Catholics. As expressed by the chief economic planner of the 1960s, discrimination was seen as 'rational' to the preservation of Northern Ireland itself:

> Catholics may not be thought to be so fully committed to performing conscientious work in a state of which they disapprove. That is to say, loyalty may be regarded as a relevant consideration even in peaceful conditions, and could be thought crucially important by employers in particularly vulnerable positions when the IRA is conducting an all-out campaign. Religious affiliation ... could then be used as a crude method of security screening in order to exclude possible IRA sympathisers

or persons who, though not sympathetic, might be intimidated into providing the terrorists with helpful information.[79]

But 'employment on the basis of merit' was never likely to be sufficient to compensate for past patterns of economic development, segmented labour markets and continued use of the most 'traditional' of all exclusions – violence and intimidation in the workplace.[80] In the Poverty and Social Exclusion survey, the equivalent of 28,000 households reported that they had been forced to leave a job because of attack, intimidation or harassment.[81]

Although the unemployment differential between Catholics and Protestants has narrowed over the past decade, workplaces remain significantly segregated.[82] Only recently has the goal of 'good relations' become a concern for public sector employers. As observed above, differences in unemployment have become less important as overall unemployment rates have fallen. One assessment points out that:

> Protestants are now underrepresented in parts of the public sector, such as education and health ... [T]he poor educational performance of the Protestant working class remains a concern, and the continued emigration of highly educated Protestant young people is likely to have a negative impact on the Protestant community's future access to higher level jobs ...[83]

Throughout the conflict the 'security industry' provided expanding employment opportunities for Protestants. In real terms, expenditure on security almost doubled between 1984 and 1994 and seemed to bear no relation to objective measures of threat. As in armed conflicts throughout the world, Northern Ireland developed a war economy. Up to 38,000 people were directly employed in the security forces and prisons at one stage, a figure that does not include security-related occupations. One estimate suggests that up to a quarter of the full-time workforce became dependent on the war economy at one stage.[84] In 1990 nearly 27 per cent of all Protestant male public-sector workers were employed in the security sector. By 2001 this figure had risen to 34 per cent, principally as a result of the decline in other public-sector employment opportunities.[85]

Loyalist and republican armed groups, based in the most economically marginalised urban and rural areas, developed sizeable 'shadow' economies, sometimes assisted by the payment of informers and agents.[86] The Glover Report suggested that the IRA's annual income was £4.5 million in the late 1970s. Ten years later it was thought to be in the region of £10 million.[87]

Most appraisals of the economic condition of Northern Ireland deal with the conflict at a very general level, if at all. Violence and the lack of stable political institutions are treated as background factors that shape business confidence and make it more difficult to attract inward investment. The precise effect of the conflict on the migration of skilled/educated labour force, capital flight and investment decisions across sectors and places remains under-researched.[88] One report suggested that 46,000 manufacturing jobs were lost because of the conflict between 1973 and 1993.[89] Most economists agree that the conflict has helped to sustain the dominance of the public sector in Northern Ireland's economy, thereby reducing the urgency of indigenous business development and interest in the role of the 'third sector' or 'social economy'.

The destruction of infrastructure is an important aspect of most armed conflicts but this was limited in the Northern Ireland case. At one stage, 160 border roads were permanently closed by the British army.[90] The North/South electricity interconnector was broken and not repairable for many years. Minor damage was frequently inflicted on the Belfast/Dublin railway track. But most of the infrastructural concerns were about a failure to develop rather than destruction as such. The economic costs associated with infrastructure problems typically arose from the extra time involved in cross-border travel and moving around Northern Ireland itself.

There have been few attempts to assess the overall financial costs of the conflict. In 1993 the House of Commons research department calculated the 'total cost of the emergency' as £14.5 billion.[91] This was a very basic measure of compensation costs, a proportion of the overall law and order budget of the Northern Ireland Office and the 'additional costs' to the British army of its role in the conflict. In other words, no allowances were made for conflict costs falling on other services – housing, health, social services, and, in particular, social security provision in respect of unemployment and incapacity. Nor was there any attempt to analyse how conflict costs were distributed between private households, the voluntary sector, business and commerce, and the public sector.

Sticking to those direct conflict costs that can be estimated with confidence, the total financial cost of the conflict was a minimum of £23.5 billion by 1993/4.[92] On a per capita basis, the conflict cost everyone in Britain the equivalent of £427, or £4,300 for every person in Ireland, North and South.

This estimate takes account of costs occurring outside of Northern Ireland. About 10.5 per cent of the total was incurred in the South and a further 7.5 per cent in Britain. As the pattern of the conflict changed in the late 1980s and early 1990s, more of the costs were borne outside of Northern Ireland – up to 30 per cent of the costs fell in Britain in the early 1990s and about 12 per cent in the South.[93] These 'regional effects' are very much in line with the international experience. The conflict drew the Irish and British governments into close contact and into a shared view at very least that the Northern conflict had to be contained as far as possible within Northern Ireland. Accordingly, policing and prison budgets rose south of the border.

Conclusion

This chapter has described the nature and extent of poverty and inequality which exists on the island of Ireland and has analysed the impact of the conflict principally in Northern Ireland. The extent of poverty was shown to be high on a number of different measures. Similarly, the levels of inequality of income, wealth and health are considerable. Indeed, Ireland and the UK now rank among the most unequal societies in the EU. The social and economic impact of the conflict has also been described. In the next chapter we explore the complex relationship between poverty and conflict in Northern Ireland using data from the PSENI study.

[1] Government of Ireland (1997) *Sharing in Progress: National Anti-Poverty Strategy*, Dublin: The Stationery Office.

[2] Department of Work and Pensions (2003) *Measuring Child Poverty*, London: DWP.

3 OFM/DFM (2001) *Programme for Government: Northern Ireland Executive*, Belfast: Office of the First Minister and Deputy First Minister. http://www.ofmdfmni.gov.uk/publications/pfga/ch1.htm

4 Noble, M. et al. (2001) *Measures of Deprivation in Northern Ireland*, Report commissioned by NISRA, Oxford: Oxford University: Social Disadvantage Research Centre. http://www.nisra.gov.uk/whatsnew/ dep/Measures%20of%20Deprivation%20for%20Northern%20Ireland% 20(28th%20June).pdf

5 Hillyard, P. et al. (2003) *Bare Necessities: Poverty and Social Exclusion in Northern Ireland – key findings*, Belfast: Democratic Dialogue.

6 Gordon, D. et al. (2000) *Poverty and social exclusion in Britain*, York: Joseph Rowntree Foundation.

7 For further details see: http://www.ark.ac.uk/nihps/

8 Hookham, S. (2004) 'Poverty, Income and Gender in Northern Ireland', unpublished M.Sc. thesis, University of Ulster.

9 A statistical adjustment using different weights is made to the household income based on the number of individuals in a household so that different incomes can be compared on an equivalent basis.

10 Nolan, B. et al. (2002) *Monitoring Poverty Trends in Ireland: Results from the 2001 Living in Ireland Survey,* Dublin: Economic and Social Research Institute.

11 OFM/DFM (2003) *New TSN Research: Poverty in Northern Ireland*, Belfast: Office of the First Minister and Deputy First Minister. http://www.research.ofmdfmni.gov.uk/povertyfull/exsummary.htm

12 This figure and those that follow are based on unpublished data from the Poverty and Social Exclusion Northern Ireland study (PSENI).

13 Pringle, D. G. et al. (2000) *Comparative Spatial Deprivation in Ireland: A Cross-Border Analysis*, Monaghan: ADM/CPA/NIVT.

14 Tomlinson, M. (2002) 'Unemployment and "Inactivity": Comparing Ireland, North and South' in Yeates, N. (ed.) *Poverty and Social Security: Comparing Ireland North and South*, Belfast: Department for Social Development, pp. 9–18.

15 Ibid., pp. 9–18.

16 All the 1991 figures quoted here are taken from O'Dowd, L., Moore, T. and Corrigan, J. (1994) *The Irish Border Region: a socio-economic profile*, Belfast: School of Sociology and Social Policy, Queen's University.

17 Calculated from 2001 Northern Ireland Census data.

18 Shuttleworth, I. and Green, A. (2004) 'A Place Apart? The Northern Ireland labour market in a wider context', in R. Osborne and I. Shuttleworth, *Fair Employment in Northern Ireland: a generation on*, Belfast: Blackstaff Press, p. 118.

[19] CORI (2004) *Socio-Economic Review: Priorities for Fairness*, Dublin: CORI, pp. 38–39. http://www.cori.ie/justice/soc_issues/inc_dist.htm

[20] Ibid., p. 32.

[21] Commission of the European Union (2003) *Commission Staff Working Paper, Draft Joint Inclusion Report*, Statistical Annex, [com (2003)773 Final], Brussels: Commission of the European Union, p. 14.

[22] OECD and Statistics Canada (2000) *Literacy in the Information Age*, Final Report of the International Adult Literacy Survey, p. 136; O'Toole, F. (2003) *After the Ball*, Dublin: New Island, p. 71.

[23] Amárach Consulting (2002) *Quality of Life in Ireland: a study for Guinness UDV Ireland*, Dublin: Amárach Consulting, pp. 10–11.

[24] Marsden, N., Woods, M. and McClelland A. (2004) *Indicators of Social Need for Northern Ireland*, Belfast: OFM/DFM, p. 73.

[25] Hillyard, P. et al. (2003) op cit. p. 43.

[26] Goodman, A. and Oldfield, Z. (2004) *Permanent Differences? Income and Expenditure Inequality in the 1990s and 2000s*, London: Institute for Fiscal Studies.

[27] It is significant that there is very little analysis of the differences between people in Northern Ireland. Far more attention is paid to the differences between Northern Ireland and Britain.

[28] Department of Enterprise Trade and Investment (2003) *Northern Ireland New Earnings Survey, 2003*, Belfast: DETI, p. 8.

[29] Ibid. p. 19.

[30] See for example Public Health Alliance Ireland (2004) *Health in Ireland: An Unequal State*, Dublin: PHAI; http://www.publichealthalliance ireland.org/PHA%20Report%20Inside%20Text%20(Final)%2010%20 June%2004.pdf; McWhirter, L., (ed.) (2004) *Equality and Inequality in Health and Social Care in Northern Ireland: A Statistical Overview*, Belfast: Department of Health, Social Services and Public Safety; http://www.dhsspsni.gov.uk/publications/2004/equality_inequalities/equ ality_inequalities.asp

[31] Ibid., PHAI (2004) op. cit.

[32] Chief Medical Officer (1999) *The Health of the Public in Northern Ireland, Report of the Chief Medical Officer*, Belfast: DHSSPS, p. 19. http://www.dhsspsni.gov.uk/publications/archived/2000/cmo99con intro.pdf.

[33] Uren, Z. et al. (2001) 'Geographic variation in mortality by Social Class and alternative social classifications', in C. Griffiths and J. Fitzpatrick (eds.) *Geographic Variations in Health*, London: Stationery Office, p. 343.

[34] Miller, R., Devine, P. and Schubotz, D. (2003) *Secondary Analysis of the 1997 and 2001 Northern Ireland Health and Social Wellbeing Surveys*, Belfast: ARK and Institute of Governance, Public Policy and Social Research, p. 23.

35 Ibid., p. 23. The authors are wrong to suggest that age is excluded under section 75. It is one of the nine dimensions.

36 Women's Human Rights Alliance (2004) *CEDAW Shadow Report on Ireland, 2004*, Women's Human Rights Alliance, p.8. http:www.whra-ireland.org/PDFs/ireland.pdf

37 Marsden, N. et al. (2004) op cit.

38 *The Cork Examiner* (2003) 'North's politicians need to work on making a better case for themselves', 31 July.

39 Department of Finance and Personnel (2002) *Review of Rating Policy: A Consultation Document, May 2002*, Belfast: Department of Finance and Personnel, Annex 4.

40 *Northern Ireland Housing Statistics, 2003–2004*, Belfast: Department for Social Development, p. 4.

41 Hillyard, P. et al. (2003) op. cit. p. 58.

42 We are most grateful to Agnieszka Martynowicz for researching this issue and to a number of people in transport departments in Northern Ireland and England.

43 Wilkinson, R. and Marmot, M. (2003) *The Solid Facts: Social Determinants of Health* (2nd edn.), Denmark: WHO.

44 Wilkinson, R. (1996) *Unhealthy Societies: The Afflictions of Inequality*, London: Routledge.

45 Dorling, D. (2004) 'Prime Suspect: murder in Britain', in Hillyard, P. et al. (eds.) *Beyond Criminology: Taking Harm Seriously*, London: Pluto, pp. 178–191.

46 See for example Lynch, J. W. et al. (2000) 'Income inequality and mortality: importance to health of individual income, psychosocial environment, or material conditions', *British Medical Journal*, 29 April, pp. 1200–1204.

47 See for example Cameron, Lord (1969) *Disturbances in Northern Ireland, Report of the Commisssion appointed by the Governor of Northern Ireland*, Belfast: HMSO; Smith, D. and Chambers, G. (1991) *Inequality in Northern Ireland*, Oxford: Oxford University Press.

48 McWhirter, L. (ed.) (2004) *Equality and Inequality in Health and Social Care in Northern Ireland: A Statistical Overview*, Belfast: Department of Health, Social Services and Public Safety.

49 Wilson, R. and Cairns, E. (1996) 'Coping processes and emotions in relation to political violence in Northern Ireland', in G. Mulhearn and S. Joseph (eds.) *Psychosocial perspectives on stress and trauma: from disaster to political violence*, Leicester: British Psychological Press, pp. 19–28; Wilson, R. and Cairns, E. (1992) 'Troubles, Stress and Psychological Disorder in Northern Ireland', *The Psychologist* 5 (8), pp. 347–350; Cairns, E. (1996) *Children and Political Violence*, Oxford: Blackwell.

50 Smyth, M. (1999) *Northern Ireland's troubles: the human costs*, London: Pluto Press.

51 Miller et al. (2003) op. cit., p. 62.

52 The General Health Questionnaire (GHQ12) is a measure of mental health and is widely used in social surveys. It is based on 12 items.

53 Miller et al. (2003) op. cit., p. 65. See also O'Reilly, D. and Stevenson, O. (2003) 'Mental Health in Northern Ireland: have "the Troubles" made it worse?' *Journal of Epidemiology and Community Health*, 57, 488–492.

54 Northern Ireland Association for Mental Health, in collaboration with the Sainsbury Council for Mental Health (2004) *Counting the Cost: the Economic and Social Costs of Mental Illness in Northern Ireland*. http://image.guardian.co.uk/sys-files/Society/documents/2004/06/08/Nimentalcosts.pdf

55 National Advisory Committee on Drugs (NACD) and Drug and Alcohol Information and Research Unit (DAIRU) (2003) *Drug Use in Ireland & Northern Ireland, First Results from the 2002/2003 Drug Prevalence Survey*, Bulletin 1, October.

56 Over the ten-year period 1989–1999, there was a 5.7 fold increase in the volume of prescribed antidepressants. See Kelly, C. B. et al. (2003) 'Antidepressant prescribing and suicide rate in Northern Ireland', *European Psychiatry*, 18 (7), 325–328.

57 BBC Northern Ireland News, 7 August 2002. http://news.bbc.co.uk/1/hi/northern_ireland/2177247.stm

58 The statistics that follow are all taken from the Samaritans' website: http://www.samaritans.org.uk

59 Crowley, P., Kilroe, J. and Burke, S. (2004) *Youth Suicide Prevention*, Dublin: Institute of Public Health and Health Development Agency.

60 'Gassing the Truth', interview with Jim McCann, Relatives for Justice. http://www.relativesforjustice.com/publications/crgas.htm; also Porton Down Veterans Support Group, www.portonveterans.8m.com/page15.html; Porter, S. (1994) 'Unhealthy Surveillance: Investigating Public Health in South Armagh', *Critical Public Health*.

61 Office for National Statistics (2003) *Regional Trends 37*, London: ONS; Central Statistics Office, *Vital Statistics*. http://www.cso.ie/

62 In both loyalist and republican neighbourhoods, alternative transport systems based on shared taxis developed. The West Belfast Taxis, in particular, became a major service. See O'Hearn, D. and Tomlinson. M. (2001) *West Belfast Taxis Research Project, Final Report*, Belfast: School of Sociology and Social Policy, Queen's University.

63 Hillyard, P. et al. (2003) op. cit., p. 59.

64 Ralaheen Ltd Dublin and EXPAC Monaghan and Strategem (forthcoming 2005) *Belfast People Displaced as a Result of the Conflict in the Southern Border Countries*. ADM/CPA.

[65] Darby, J. and Morris, G. (1974) *Intimidation in housing*, Belfast: Northern Ireland Community Relations Commission.

[66] Hillyard, P. et al. (2003) op. cit., p. 62.

[67] Northern Ireland Affairs Committee (2001) *Relocation Following Paramilitary Intimidation*, London: Stationery Office, HC 59-I.

[68] Memorandum of Evidence to Northern Ireland Affairs Committee, 13 December 2000.

[69] *Hansard*, HC (Session 2002–03), vol. 405, written answers, col. 677 (20 May 2003).

[70] Holden McAllister Partnership (2003) *The Needs of Exiles,* Part 2 of *The Legacy, a study of the needs of GB victims and survivors of the Northern Ireland 'Troubles'*, Nottingham: The Tim Parry Jonathan Ball Trust, p. 128.

[71] Segregated means that the estate was at least 90 per cent Catholic or Protestant. See Jarman, N. (2002) *Managing Disorder, Responding to Interface Violence in North Belfast*, Belfast: OFM/DFM.

[72] Ibid., p. 16.

[73] Murtagh, B. (2002) *The Politics of Territory, Policy and Segregation in Northern Ireland*, London: Palgrave.

[74] *Hansard*, HC (Session 2001–02), vol. 376, col. 220w (4 December 2001).

[75] Connolly, P., Smith, A. and Kelly, B. (2002) *Too Young to Notice? The Cultural and Political Awareness of 3–6 Year Olds in Northern Ireland*, Belfast: Northern Ireland Community Relations Council, p. 5.

[76] Only about 5 per cent of children attend integrated schools. Ibid., p. 5.

[77] Sheehan, M. and Tomlinson, M. (1999) *The Unequal Unemployed: Discrimination, unemployment and state policy in Northern Ireland*, Aldershot: Ashgate.

[78] *Economic Bulletin*, 10 (2), Belfast: West Belfast Economic Forum, November 2003.

[79] Wilson, T. (1989) *Ulster: Conflict and Consent*, Oxford: Basil Blackwell, p. 109.

[80] McVeigh, R. and Fisher, C. (2002) *Chill Factor or Kill Factor? The effects of sectarian intimidation on employment in West Belfast*, Belfast: West Belfast Economic Forum; Sheehan, M. and Tomlinson, M. (1999) op. cit., pp. 105–107.

[81] Hillyard, P. et al. (2003) op. cit., p. 62.

[82] Shirlow, P. (2003) 'Religious Discrimination and Beyond', *Economic Bulletin*, 10 (2), 23–24.

[83] Shuttleworth, I. and Osborne, R. (2004) 'Concluding Remarks', in R. Osborne and I. Shuttleworth *Fair Employment in Northern Ireland: a generation on*, Belfast: Blackstaff Press, p. 188.

[84] Tomlinson, M. (1994) *25 Years On: The Costs of War and the Dividends of Peace*, Belfast: West Belfast Economic Forum, p. 14.

[85] Russell, R. (2004) 'Employment profiles of Protestants and Catholics', in B. Osborne and I. Shuttleworth (eds.) *Fair Employment in Northern Ireland: A generation on*, Belfast: Blackstaff Press.

[86] At the height of the conflict hundreds of people were receiving payments at any one time. In the calendar year 2000, a total of £176,580 was paid out to informers. *Hansard*, HC (Session 2001–02), vol. 375, written answers, col. 1074 (29 November 2001).

[87] Maguire, K. (1993) 'Policing the Black Economy: the role of C13 of the RUC in Northern Ireland', *The Police Journal*, April, p. 134.

[88] The New Ireland Forum estimated that 40,000 manufacturing jobs had been lost to the conflict between 1969 and 1982.

[89] DKM Economic Consultants (1994) *The Economic Impact of the Northern Ireland Conflict*, Dublin: DKM, p. 32.

[90] Tomlinson, M. (1993) 'Policing the New Europe: the Northern Ireland Factor', in T. Bunyan (ed.) *Statewatching the New Europe*, London: Statewatch, pp. 95–96

[91] *Hansard*, HC (Session 1992–93), vol. 230, col. 515 (22 October 1993).

[92] Tomlinson, M. (1994) op. cit., p. 32.

[93] Ibid., p. 32.

Chapter 5

The Relationship between Poverty and Conflict in Northern Ireland

Introduction

The suggestion that there is an association between violent conflict in Ireland and poverty/deprivation has a range of meanings. In this chapter, we explore the extent to which acts of violence have been concentrated in poor or deprived areas or disproportionately experienced by poor households, based on data for Northern Ireland. The poverty-conflict relationship is explored at the spatial level and in relation to individuals. The former involves an analysis of the spatial distribution of violent incidents and the extent to which they are associated with poor areas defined by some deprivation index, such as the Robson, Noble or Townsend indices. The latter involves a survey of a random sample of people who are asked about their experiences of the conflict. These data are then examined to ascertain the extent to which experiences are concentrated in poor households. There are problems with both approaches.

The location of violence

To begin with, the methods of warfare used by the protagonists in the conflict in Northern Ireland have differed and have had different effects on different sections of the population, thus obscuring the precise relationship between violence, conflict and poverty. The IRA, for example, made extensive use of car-bombings in centres of towns and cities. The bombings mainly took place in better-off areas, with those killed and injured coming from a fairly broad cross-section of the population. Thus neither a spatial analysis nor a survey is likely to find a strong relationship between the experience or witnessing of bombings and poverty. The IRA also carried out numerous shooting attacks on members of the army and the police. Many of the shootings took place in poorer areas but those killed came from a range of backgrounds. Some came from outside of Northern Ireland; others, like members of the police, came mostly from the middle-class Protestant community. Thus while a spatial analysis of the shootings may show a strong relationship between violence and poverty, an analysis based on a survey of individual experiences may not.

The relationship is further compounded by the methods adopted by loyalist paramilitaries. They focused mainly on killing Catholics at random. Although many of the killings took place at interface areas that experience high levels of poverty, middle-class members of the Catholic community and a number of Protestants who were 'mis-identified' were also assassinated. Once again, these patterns of violent incidents distort any relationship between poverty and violence. Finally, the proactive and reactive methods adopted by the security forces, which led to many deaths and injuries of armed and unarmed combatants as well as civilians, would further compound the complexity of the relationship between violence and poverty, whichever way it is measured.

There is a further problem associated with the spatial analysis – the ecological fallacy. This situation can occur when an inference is made about an individual based on the aggregate data. For example, it may be found that a particular area has a very high rate of violent incidents. It is then assumed that all people in the area have experienced the high rate. But on closer examination it is clear that most of the violent incidents have taken place in, say, one estate and people outside of the estate have been relatively unaffected by the violence. Great care therefore needs to be taken in using aggregate data as it may conceal a number of crucial variations.

The Cost of the Troubles Study analysed the experience and impact of the conflict in Northern Ireland.[1] The consequences for adults were investigated in a large survey of some 3,000 people drawn from a random sample of 30 wards stratified by death rates from political violence in each ward over the last 30 years. Wards that had been at the centre of the conflict were, therefore, over-represented. The impact on young people was explored separately and involved interviews with 85 youngsters. The adult survey found that location and religion stood as the two most significant determinants of the degree of exposure and the amount of effects experienced as a result of the conflict. While the study did not attempt to explore systematically the relationship between conflict and poverty, it did find that those wards that had experienced the highest intensity of violence contained more households with extremely low incomes and high benefits dependency. In addition, the study compared the death rates for particular locations and compared them with deprivation scores based on the Robson Index. It found that of the six districts that ranked highest on fatal incidents, four were among the six most deprived. Although both sources – the survey and the area database – suggest an association between violence and poverty, it is difficult to ascertain whether the relationship is significant in the survey data because of over-sampling or an ecological fallacy in the case of the death database.

The experience of violence

The PSENI study, which was carried out in 2002/2003, was based on a representative sample of 3,164 individuals, following a response rate of 64 per cent.[2] The principal aim was to construct a robust measurement of poverty, and the main findings on the nature and extent of poverty have been discussed in Chapter 4. A number of question modules were asked of randomly chosen sub-samples of people on the following topics: area characteristics, community support, activism, local services, mobility, and the conflict. In the last module people were asked about their experience of seven conflict-related events: whether they knew someone who had been killed or injured in the conflict, whether they had witnessed various traumatic events, such as a bomb explosion or a murder, or whether they had been forced to move house or job due to attack, intimidation, threats or harassment. A total of 1,649 people answered questions relating to these events.

The impact of the conflict on people in Northern Ireland has been extensive. Overall, 49 per cent of individuals said they knew someone who had been killed in the conflict. Of those affected by a death, some 14 per cent had lost a close relative, 25 per cent a close friend and 39 per cent someone else. In terms of injury, nearly 8 per cent had been injured themselves. Twenty-six per cent knew a friend who had been injured, some 17 per cent a relative, and over a third someone else. In addition, some 8 per cent of people were forced to move house and 5 per cent a job because of an attack, intimidation, threats or harassment.

The incidence of people experiencing various conflict-related events was explored in relation to a number of different groups (see Figures 5.1 to 5.6). Age was statistically significant (see note below) on six of the seven events, with the 35–44 and 45–54 age groups having higher proportions of people knowing someone who was killed or injured in most of the categories compared with their numbers in the population as a whole. Most of the other age groups scored less on most of the incidents. Gender too was statistically significant on six of the seven events, with men much more likely than women to have known someone who was killed or injured during the conflict. Another important variable was the tenure of the household. Respondents in housing executive owned houses were much more likely to know someone who had been killed or injured than people living in other types of tenure. Finally, there were differences between Catholic and Protestant communities. On all but one measure Catholics knew a higher proportion of people killed or injured than Protestants. However, the differences were significant on only three of the seven items and then only at the 5 per cent confidence level.

Note:
In the following charts, levels of significance are recorded as: * = <.05, ** = <.01, *** = <.001 where, for example, ** means that we can be 99 percent certain that the result does not occur by chance.

Figure 5.1 Incidence of people knowing someone killed or injured during the conflict by age

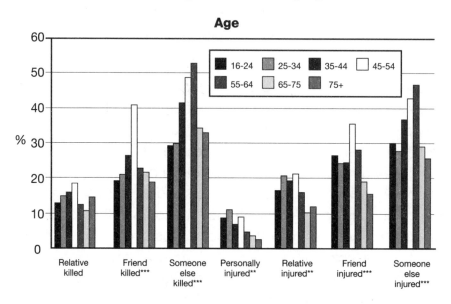

Figure 5.2 Incidence of people knowing someone killed or injured during the conflict by gender

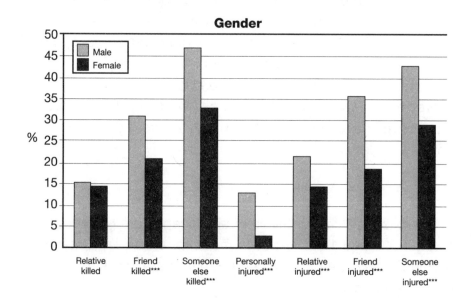

Figure 5.3 Incidence of people knowing someone killed or injured during the conflict by religion

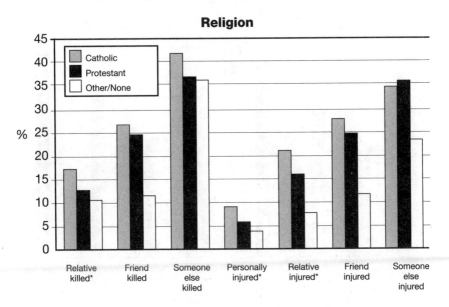

Figure 5.4 Incidence of people knowing someone killed or injured during the conflict by household type

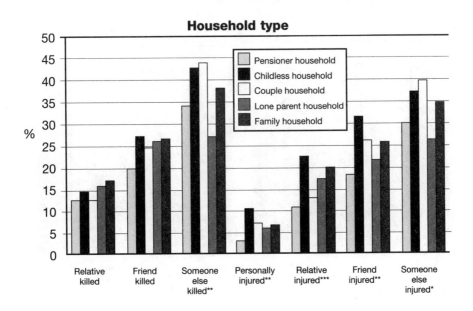

Figure 5.5 Incidence of people knowing someone killed or injured during the conflict by tenure

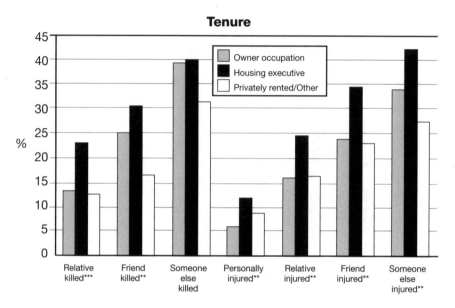

Figure 5.6 Incidence of people knowing someone killed or injured during the conflict by social class

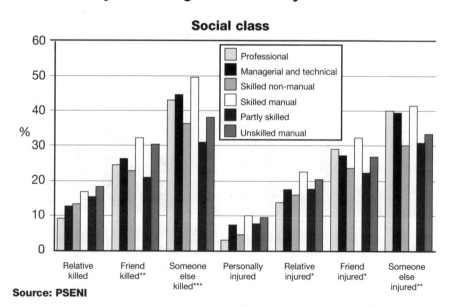

Source: PSENI

A composite index was constructed to indicate the respondent's association with the total number of people killed. This showed that some 26 per cent knew of one person, 17 per cent two people and some 6 per cent three people. A further index, which combined both killings and injuries, was also constructed. It again illustrates the extent to which the impact of the conflict was differentiated by age. The age group most affected by the conflict was the 45–54 age group who had knowledge of on average 2.2 killings or injuries. There was also an important gender division with men knowing on average 2 killings or injuries compared with women who on average knew of 1.3. The average number of incidents for Catholics was 1.8 and for Protestants 1.5; for house owners it was 1.6, for housing executive tenants 2.0 and for respondents who rent houses privately 1.3.

As well as killings and injuries, the survey explored the extent to which people had witnessed violent incidents. Nearly 60 per cent of individuals had witnessed one or more of six listed violent incidents: a bomb explosion, a murder, gunfire, rioting, someone being assaulted, or other serious violence. This is a higher proportion than the 49 per cent who knew someone who had been killed or injured. Over 34 per cent of respondents had witnessed a bomb explosion, 26 per cent gunfire, 38 per cent rioting, 21 per cent someone being assaulted and 5 per cent someone being murdered.

Figures 5.7 to 5.12 show the incidence of people witnessing violent events during the conflict. Once again age was statistically significant for all events. However, the age groups varied according to the particular event. For example, the 35-44 year olds were most likely to have witnessed a bomb explosion, murder or gunfire, whereas the 25-34 age group were more likely to have witnessed rioting and the 16-24 age group someone being assaulted. Gender was again statistically significant on all events, with men witnessing a higher proportion of each event than women. In relation to religion, Catholics witnessed a higher proportion of all violent events than Protestants but the differences were statistically significant only for gunfire, someone being assaulted and other serious violence. Household type was statistically significant for four of the six events, with households without children and lone parents experiencing the highest incidence. Finally, tenure was statistically significant for three of the seven events.

Figure 5.7 Incidence of people witnessing violent events during the conflict by age

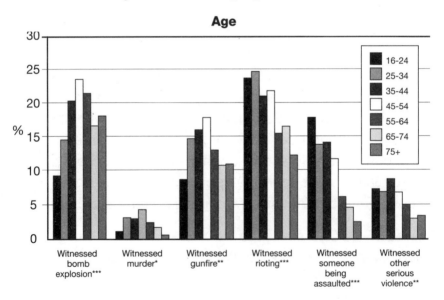

Figure 5.8 Incidence of people witnessing violent events during the conflict by gender

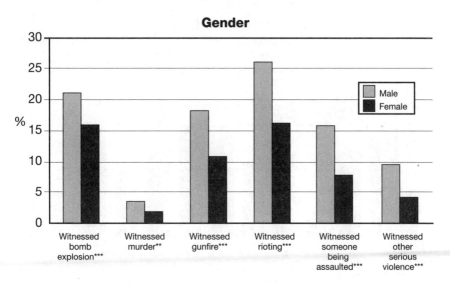

Figure 5.9 Incidence of people witnessing violent events during the conflict by religion

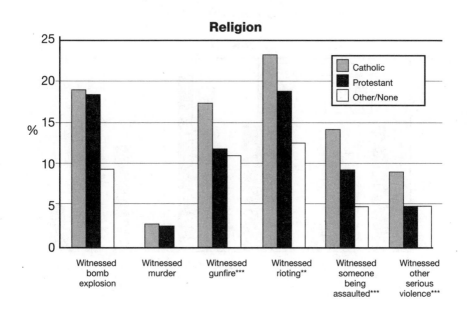

Figure 5.10 Incidence of people witnessing violent events during the conflict by household type

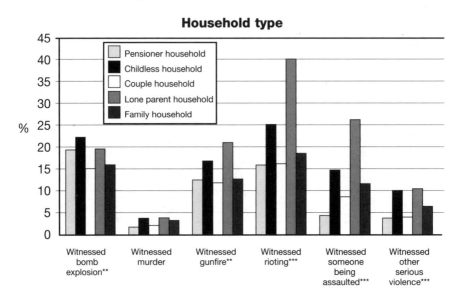

Household type

Figure 5.11 Incidence of people witnessing violent events during the conflict by tenure

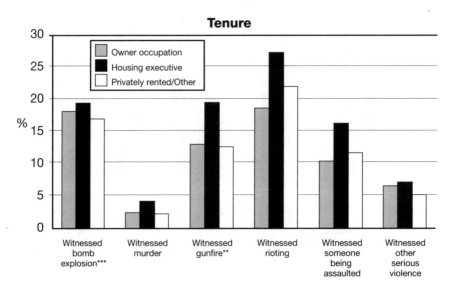

Tenure

Figure 5.12 Incidence of people witnessing violent events during the conflict by social class

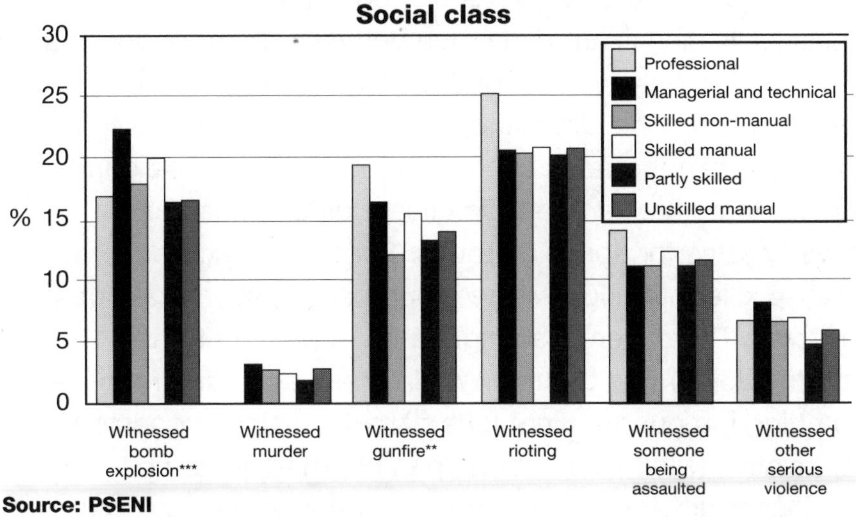

Source: PSENI

Using an index of the number of violent events witnessed, 37 per cent of respondents witnessed one or two incidents and 22 per cent witnessed three or more events. Forty-one per cent had witnessed no violent incident.

Poverty rates for people experiencing violence

The key question for this report is to what extent experiences of violence are related to poverty. Overall, the survey calculated on the basis of a consensual definition of poverty that 30 per cent of Northern Ireland households were poor. Although it has been shown that housing executive tenants, who are three and a half times more likely to be at risk of poverty than owner occupiers, have a significantly higher proportion of respondents experiencing a selected event (for example, personal injury, a relative killed, a friend killed or injured), there is no clear pattern.

Figures 5.13 and 5.14 show the poverty rates for persons knowing someone killed or injured or witnessing violent events during the conflict. As can be seen there is a statistically significant difference between the poor and the non-poor on only two out of the seven experiences of knowing someone killed and four of the seven witnessed events. When the rates are broken down by age, sex and tenure, there are very few significant differences in the poverty rates for specific groups. For those who had a relative killed, the 45–54 age group had a poverty rate of 44 per cent. There were also high rates of poverty for the 16–24 and the 25–34 age groups. Within these two age groups combined, a quarter were lone parents, which suggests that the relative killed was another parent. There were no significant differences, however, between tenure groups.

Figure 5.13 Poverty rates for persons knowing someone killed or injured during the conflict

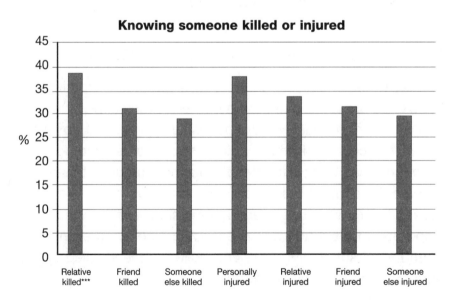

Figure 5.14 Poverty rates for persons witnessing violent events during the conflict

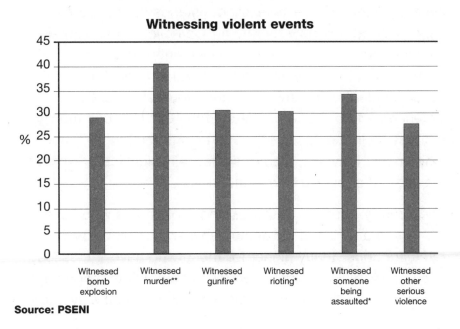

Witnessing violent events

Source: PSENI

The absence of any clear relationship between knowing someone killed or injured or witnessing violent events and poverty may be related to the different forms of warfare which the two communities perpetuated and experienced. It is therefore important to explore the relationship between violence and poverty separately for each of the two communities.

Overall, the levels of poverty varied between the two communities. The poverty rate for Catholics was 36 per cent while the rate for Protestants was 25 per cent. Figures 5.15 and 5.16 show the poverty rates for people knowing someone killed or injured or witnessing a violent event broken down by religion. Two features stand out. First, the poverty rates for Catholics are consistently greater than for

Protestants for each category. In four of the seven listed violent events the poverty rate is over 40 per cent and in one instance – that of a relative killed – stands at over 50 per cent. Second, the poverty rate for Catholics exceeds their average rate of 36 per cent in all incidents, while for Protestants it exceeds their average rate in only three of the seven incidents. These figures, therefore, suggest that violence and poverty are related in the Catholic community but less so in the case of the Protestant community. The differences, however, are not statistically significant except in the case of a relative or a friend killed.

The poverty rates for Catholics and Protestants who have witnessed a series of incidents again show that Catholic rates are consistently higher for those who have witnessed each of the major incidents. In the case of witnessing four out of the seven incidents the rates are higher than the average

Figure 5.15 Poverty rates for persons knowing someone killed or injured during the conflict by religion

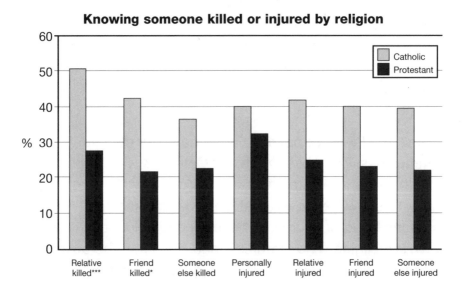

Figure 5.16 Poverty rates for persons witnessing violent events during the conflict by religion

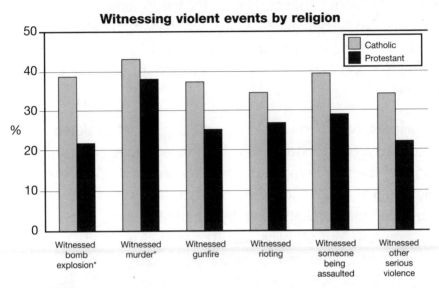

Source: PSENI

poverty rate for the Catholic community. In the Protestant community a similar relationship appears to exist for a number of incidents. For example, the poverty rate for Protestants who have witnessed a murder is 38 per cent – some 14 percentage points above the poverty rate for the Protestant community overall. A similar pattern is observable for rioting and assault, although not to such an extent. These figures again suggest that for the Catholic community poverty is related to experience of violence but the differences are statistically significant in only three of the seven incidents.

So far, this analysis has focused on people's experiences of individual events. But people may have experienced more than one of the events and hence the trauma for them will possibly be greater than for someone who has experienced only one. It is therefore important to capture the depth of the experience to see if it is associated with poverty. To explore this idea further, an index was developed of extreme violence that combined the most serious types of violence: killings (relative), injuries (self and relative) and witnessing an incident (murder). Just over 10 per cent of people had experience of two or more of these four events.

This index of extreme violence was significantly related to poverty. Respondents who had experienced two or more of the four items had a poverty rate of 43 per cent. Figures 5.17–5.22 show the poverty rates for the extreme violence index broken down by different groups. The poverty rate for Catholics was 51 per cent and for Protestants 33 per cent. This selective approach shows unequivocally that violence and poverty are clearly related. More importantly, those who have experienced two or more events are disproportionately concentrated in housing executive dwellings, the 45–54 year age group, and in single households. They experience greater levels of medium and high stress as measured on five General Health Questions.

Those who experienced intimidation in the workplace and were forced to leave their jobs had significantly raised poverty rates. In the case of Catholics intimidated out of work the poverty rate was 55 per cent and for Protestants 31 per cent. The poverty rate for Protestants forced to move house was 38 per cent compared to the Catholic rate of 48 per cent. Experience of intimidation was associated with slighter higher poverty rates than for imprisonment or knowing someone who had served time because of the conflict.

Figure 5.17 Poverty rates for people experiencing two or more of the four most serious incidents of violence by age

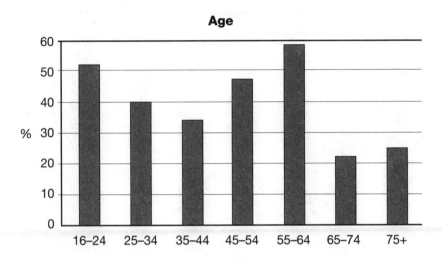

Figure 5.18 Poverty rates for people experiencing two or more of the four most serious incidents of violence by gender

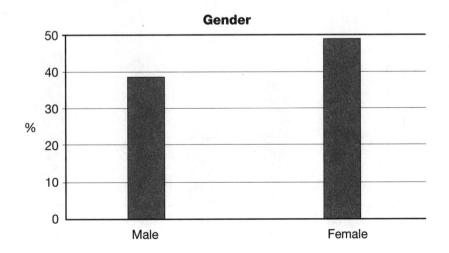

Figure 5.19 Poverty rates for people experiencing two or more of the four most serious incidents of violence by religion

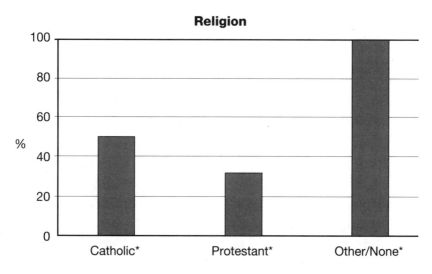

Figure 5.20 Poverty rates for people experiencing two or more of the four most serious incidents of violence by household type

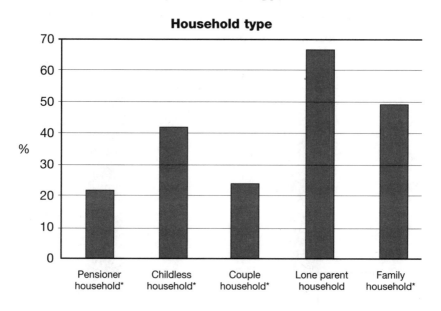

Figure 5.21 Poverty rates for people experiencing two or more of the four most serious incidents of violence by tenure

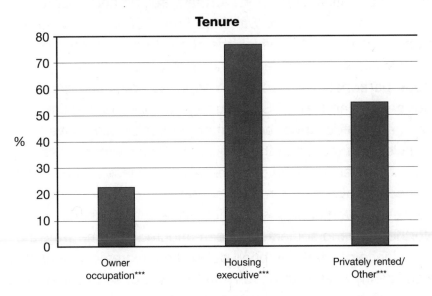

Figure 5.22 Poverty rates for people experiencing two or more of the four most serious incidents of violence by social class

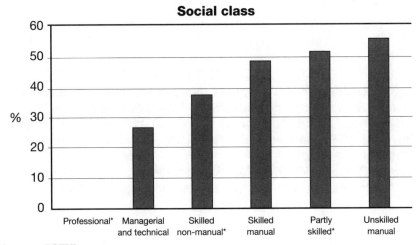

Source: PSENI

Conclusion

This chapter has explored the link between direct experience of violent political conflict in Northern Ireland and poverty. *The Cost of the Troubles Study* and the PSENI survey both highlight the extent to which the conflict has impacted on people's lives. The evidence shows that violence has disproportionately impacted on deprived areas and groups in Northern Ireland. The PSENI survey has, for the first time, been able to describe the numbers of people who have lost relatives and friends in the conflict and their experiences of violent incidents and to examine whether these features were related to poverty. The results suggest a complex relationship between poverty and the conflict. While a wide sector of Northern Ireland society has been affected in some way, the experience of what has been defined as 'extreme violence' is significantly related to poverty. In the face of such evidence it is hard to deny the importance of socio-economic factors. While they are certainly not the only factors associated with the conflict, they form an important dimension. Experience of violent conflict should therefore not be overlooked in any anti-poverty strategy.

---

[1] Fay, M. T., Morrissey, M., Smyth, M. Wong, T. (1999) *The Cost of the Troubles Study: Report on the Northern Ireland Survey: the experience and impact of the Troubles*, Derry: Incore; Fay, M.T., Morrissey, M. and Smyth, M. (1999) *Northern Ireland's Troubles: the Human Costs*, London: Pluto Press.

[2] Hillyard, P. et al. (2003) *Bare Necessities: Poverty and Social Exclusion in Northern Ireland – key findings*, Belfast: Democratic Dialogue.

Chapter 6

Reconstructing Ireland: A Lost Opportunity?

Introduction

We have argued throughout this report that the relationship between conflict and poverty is a complex one. While this precludes any easy solutions to the problems of either conflict or poverty, it does at least alert us to the fact that, in a society where both coexist, attempts to tackle one cannot be carried out in the absence of policies to counteract the other. Nowhere is this more evident than in the post-conflict or transitional phase when reconstruction is paramount. The earlier review of best international practice has identified a number of guidelines for reconstructing war-torn societies:

- Reconstruction must not confine itself simply to economic tasks but must prioritise rebuilding society socially and politically.

- Poverty reduction does not necessarily follow from economic reconstruction but must be a specific target of policy.

- Although ending conflict is a political task, it cannot take place in the absence of an attempt to eradicate the inequality that both derives from and feeds conflict.

- Unless constant care is taken, reconstruction can lead to the replication of the previous systems of power and privilege in new forms.

- An awareness of gender must be at the forefront of reconstruction, through policies that ensure the involvement of women in all aspects of transition – economic, social and political.

- Central to social reconstruction is a commitment to human rights.

- Human rights work in transitional societies involves actions such as establishing bodies to ensure a future commitment to human rights, re-training of security and judicial personnel, and dealing with the human rights abuses of the past.

- The demobilisation and reintegration of combatants, in particular those from oppositional forces, must be tackled directly if peace is to be assured. The most effective way to ensure successful demobilisation is through adequate funding of ex-combatant self-help schemes.

- The building/rebuilding of civil society requires a commitment to community development principles and practices, as well as adequate funding to sustain grass-roots activities.

- The needs of women, whether as victims, widows or ex-combatants, must be considered specifically.

- The needs of children and young people, whether as victims or perpetrators of violence, must be considered specifically.

Examples abound of valuable and effective progress when these guidelines have been followed. The purpose of this chapter is to examine the extent to which these guidelines have been applied in the Irish context, following the cease-fires.

The cease-fires of the IRA and the Combined Loyalist Military Command in 1994 represented a clear consolidation of the peace process which had been developing in previous years. They also evidenced increased involvement of the international community in the affairs of Northern Ireland. Eventually political talks led to the 1998 Agreement. In joint referenda held on 22 May 1998, 71.1 per cent of voters in Northern Ireland and 94.4 per cent in the Republic of Ireland endorsed the 1998 Agreement, an all-Ireland majority of 85.4 per cent in favour. Strand One of the 1998 Agreement dealt with the constitutional arrangements – the Assembly, Executive, Civic Forum and Cross-Border bodies. Strand Two covered the North/South Ministerial Council. Strand Three dealt with a range of matters – the British-Irish Council, British-Irish Intergovernmental Conference, Rights, Safeguards and Equality of Opportunity, Decommissioning, Security, Policing and Justice.

Many of the issues we looked at globally in Chapter 3 could be seen to fall into Strand Three in the Irish context. But the strands were designed to work together, not in isolation. In this light the failure to fully implement Strand One could prove to be a major obstacle as regards the ability to deliver on the 1998 Agreement. The institutions set up through Strand One have now been suspended on four separate occasions and currently the implementation of the 1998 Agreement as a whole is subject to a review by the two governments and all parties in the Assembly. In this context the chances of Strand

Three delivering progress on issues such as human rights and justice have been diminished.

Economic reconstruction and the peace dividend

In Chapter 3, we examined the debate on the issue of reconstruction. We noted that a number of international organisations, most notably the World Bank, approached this issue from a neo-liberal perspective. The primacy of the market is seen as the key to the solution of problems of conflict and poverty. Reconstruction is thus fundamentally a task at the economic level, and at the political level in as far as it can clear the field to allow the market to do its job. Much lower down the agenda in the neo-liberal approach to reconstruction is a concern about social and political issues, in particular, the question of human rights. The purpose here is to examine the extent to which neo-liberal ideas influenced conflict-related intervention in Ireland, North and South.

Neo-liberal intervention

British economic policy towards Northern Ireland in the 1980s ensured that the region was spared the worst effects of the Conservative government swing from Keynesianism to monetarism. While the public sector was cut back rapidly in the rest of the UK, it continued at pre-1980 levels in Northern Ireland.[1] At the same time, elements of a neo-liberal perspective did emerge in Northern Ireland. A key example is the International Fund for Ireland (IFI), established in 1985 as part of the Anglo-Irish Agreement. Money is provided mainly by the US, but also by Canada, Australia, New Zealand and the EU. The IFI spends approximately three-quarters of its resources in Northern Ireland and a quarter in the Southern border counties (Donegal, Sligo, Leitrim, Cavan, Monaghan and Louth). To date, the Fund has spent €603 million on 4,850 projects.[2]

The IFI has two stated objectives: 'to promote economic and social advances' and 'to encourage contact, dialogue and reconciliation between nationalists and unionists throughout Ireland'. From the start the Fund faced a number of criticisms: that its money was not always ending up in the areas where it was most needed; that the criteria for grant making were not always transparent and not always visibly based on social need;[3] that the priorities of the Fund were often determined by an openly political agenda of the British government, most notably in relation to the 'political vetting' of community groups.[4] The Fund took some of these criticisms on board, for example inaugurating a Special Projects (Disadvantaged Areas) programme in 1989 in order to ensure that more money was allocated to areas of greatest deprivation.

A more fundamental criticism can be made relating to the theme of reconstruction. 'Economic advance' has been defined in very specific ways by the IFI. Thus although it has disbursed money under a number of headings – such as 'Special Projects (Disadvantaged Areas)' and 'Community Relations' – there is no doubt that two headings take priority: 'Business Enterprise' and 'Community Economic Regeneration'. Within that focus, in the early days in particular, large grants were given to banks for the refurbishment of branch offices in small towns, and funding was provided for government building or infrastructural projects without any apparent commitment to a principle of additionality.[5] This policy of allocating large amounts of money to property development or pump-priming capital investment reveals a belief in a central element of neo-liberalism, the 'trickle-down' theory of development.

The neo-liberal approach has been even more apparent in the context of the 1998 Agreement. Many politicians, North and South, have voiced their conviction of the ability of the market to deliver in terms of reconstruction. For example, in the South, Michael McDowell, the Minister for Justice, Equality and Law Reform, stated: 'A dynamic liberal economy like ours demands flexibility and inequality in some respects. It is this inequality which provides incentives.' Aligned with this faith is a relegation of human rights concerns to secondary position, if not lower. Thus, Minister McDowell went on to say that 'the current rights culture and equality notion would create a feudal society'.[6] In a similar vein David Trimble, then First Minister of the Northern Ireland Executive, informed an international congress on terrorist victims in Madrid: 'One of the great curses of this world is the human rights industry. They justify terrorist acts and end up being complicit in the murder of innocent victims'.[7]

The neo-liberal focus on physical rather than social reconstruction at first sight appears anomalous in the Irish situation. The destruction of infrastructure was much less than in most other war-torn societies. At the same time, the military conflict did have infrastructural effects which clearly demanded attention once that conflict was ended. The Dublin-Belfast rail line had frequently been damaged in bomb attacks, as had North-South electricity supply lines; the British army had closed dozens of border roads, particularly in Fermanagh. Thus, some intervention at the level of physical reconstruction has occurred; the main road between Dublin and Belfast has been improved, and the Dublin-Belfast rail link is being upgraded; border roads have been reopened.

On the other hand, reconstruction has failed to deliver fully even at this technical level. Thus while there have been major improvements in cross-border travel as a result of investment by the Irish government, there has been much less investment by the authorities in Northern Ireland. In short, there has been little evidence of a robust cross-border policy of reconstruction in relation to travel.

The relatively low level of physical destruction has not prevented the development of a neo-liberal tendency to represent economic reconstruction as being central to conflict transformation in Northern Ireland. Thus the Rand Corporation has reported that Making Belfast Work and the Londonderry Initiative are 'joint denominational initiatives' which have been 'facilitating nascent cross-community linkages', that 'business interests are playing an active role in dampening prominent interfaces of sectarian tension', and that 'commercial interest groups have acted as a "brake" on both Republican and Loyalist violence by discouraging retaliatory riots and attacks'.[8] The source of these insights is identified solely as 'author interviews'. Clearly, the respondents had no information to provide about the efforts of civil society groups in the management or transformation of conflict.

Sources closer to home are less messianic, but sometimes even there the optimism is difficult to sustain. For example, in January 2003, Translink, the publicly funded bus and rail company, announced a massive £22.6 million investment in 190 new buses. The money was provided by the EU Programme for Peace and Reconciliation on the basis that: 'The monies provided by Peace II for Public Transport ... ensure that no individual or community is excluded from full participation in our society'.[9] While this is a valid expectation in any well-functioning society, it is an act of faith to conclude that 'peace', 'reconciliation' and 'full participation' can emerge simply from an overdue investment in new buses.

That some will benefit from such economic initiatives is beyond doubt. For example, some of the new buses for Translink will be supplied by Ballymena-based coach makers, Wrights, thus providing employment for workers at that firm. And cross-border roads and rail links undoubtedly benefit business and tourism and thus have effects on employment possibilities. That said, it cannot be concluded that new buses, improved electricity supply, etc., are of themselves sufficient to ensure conflict transformation, that is, the establishment of a sustainable peace to underpin economic development.

Yet faith in the ability of economic measures of themselves to transform society is frequently revealed. In November 2004, as negotiations to restore the political institutions in Northern Ireland reached a peak, the two main parties, the Democratic Unionist Party and Sinn Féin, put forward a proposal for a £1 billion peace dividend. It would appear that this was to be an 'economic regeneration programme', the details of which owe much to the suggestions of the Business Alliance, an umbrella group that included the Confederation of British Industry, the Institute of Directors, the Northern Ireland Chambers of Commerce and Industry and the Northern Ireland Centre for Competitiveness. Not surprisingly, there were proposals to write off expenditure by companies on research and development, training and marketing in order to 'encourage big multinationals to locate' and to 'compete head-to-head with the Republic's low corporation tax rate'.[10] Apart from the fact that any such programme may well do little more than offset likely budget cuts in relation to the

Northern Ireland economy, all of this is compatible with a neo-liberal model whereby development is defined solely in terms of increased multinational investment. There is no mention of increased funding for civil society or for innovative programmes in relation to social and economic justice.

Peace dividend?

Has the peace process, and the 1998 Agreement itself, resulted in a 'peace dividend'? The promise that an end to armed hostilities will bring economic and social gains is clearly important in all peace processes. Equally, the frustration of unfulfilled expectations may lead to further social and political unrest, as in South Africa, or deepening military conflict, as in Palestine.

Most attempts to answer the peace dividend question look at key economic indicators such as GDP, employment growth and unemployment rates.[11] The problem is how to judge the impact of cease-fires, as against the continuing uncertainties surrounding the political institutions. Unemployment has declined but participation rates remain stagnant. Extra spending by the EU and the IFI has multiplier effects that cannot be easily distinguished from increases in public-sector programmes such as health and education. As discussed below, security-related expenditure remains at a high level, though to what extent this is justified in terms of current threats is debatable. Occasionally, there are specific indicators of new capital flight, or at least a suspension of investment in the wake of political breakdown. But, on balance, the indications are that 'the anticipated peace dividends may have been exaggerated'.[12]

Another side to the discussion is how the peace process offers ways of stimulating and enhancing economic development through cross-border co-operation; as Democratic Dialogue puts it, 'the aim … should be to remove the border *in an economic sense*' [emphasis in the original].[13] Such an explicitly pro-business agenda would include the UK adopting the Euro, an all-Ireland inward investment agency and North/South harmonisation of taxation of transnational corporations. It would be desirable, so the argument continues, to integrate labour markets, which would involve mutual recognition of qualifications and dealing with any concerns about the portability of social insurance and pensions. Much could be done to unify postal and telecommunications charges so that the island of Ireland operates as one market. However, the only area with progress to report is transport.

The peace dividend issue cannot, however, rest on such general assessments of economic performance or wish lists about cross-border co-operation. It is also important to know how the structure of economic activity and the role of the state have changed between the outbreak of armed conflict and the emergence of the peace process. In particular, it needs to be considered whether those who benefit most during conflict end up benefiting most from a peace dividend. As O'Hearn states:

> [P]eace dividends are generally portrayed in 'win-win' terms, where whole regions will benefit from increased integration in the global economy … *Within* regions, peace processes give hope to marginalized insurgent communities … that they can achieve political, economic, and cultural equality against the prevailing privileges of the dominant community. But 'peace dividends' promise to benefit the dominant community as well, by raising hopes of prosperity in an economy

that has been restricted by conflict ... [T]his is an inherently unstable situation that has the potential to destabilize a peace process if the raised expectations of one or other of the communities are not met.[14]

We saw in Chapter 4 how the conflict was quite compatible with widening income inequalities, so it is reasonable to expect that middle- and upper-income groups will sustain and even improve their advantage in any peace dividend scenario. The prospect for individuals and communities worst affected by the conflict is that social and economic marginalisation will continue, whatever the political expectations arising from the peace process – unless, that is, there is a determined effort aimed at social and economic reconstruction.

The form of peace dividends is clearly dependent on the type of economy and level of development. Given the South's record in attracting US investment and the political interest in Northern Ireland shown by the US government under President Clinton, it was reasonable to expect that Northern Ireland would see a surge in inward investment as the principal benefit of peace. International support for Northern Ireland from EU and other funds also led to expectations that the war-torn communities could expect substantial support in other ways.

Very little research has been done on the precise impact of inward investment and other state-supported corporate investment on marginalised communities. For example, information is often provided on 'jobs promoted' rather than jobs generated by duration. One study of the impact of state-supported investment in West Belfast concluded that there was a net loss of state-supported jobs in the area from the mid-1990s:

Taking job losses and new jobs together, the number of IDB-sponsored jobs was actually 135 *fewer* at the beginning of 1999 than at the time of the cease-fire in 1994. Despite the insistent publicity offensive to the contrary, this indicates that *in terms of new employment, the promised peace dividend was actually negative.*[15]

If there are questions to be asked about the level and distribution of state-supported jobs in economically marginalised communities, there are also questions to be raised about commitments to social inclusion.

One practical way in which the states in Ireland, North and South, could do better is in relation to procurement. The Irish government spends €8.8 billion on procuring privately supplied goods, services and capital projects each year. Northern Ireland spends a further £1.5 billion. Procurement policy, except in relation to small contracts, is subject to European Directives[16] and World Trade Organisation rules. As recent debates around EU procurement rules have demonstrated, much more could be done to integrate social and environmental policy objectives, including production methods and ethical criteria, into public procurement.[17] Further, there is nothing preventing businesses from voluntarily developing trading and other links with economically marginalised areas.

Poverty reduction and conflict

The 1998 Agreement acknowledged the importance of economic growth and equality of opportunity:

> Pending the devolution of powers to a new Northern Ireland Assembly, the British Government will pursue broad policies for sustained economic growth and

stability in Northern Ireland and for promoting social inclusion, including in particular community development and the advancement of women in public life.[18]

There would be rapid progress on a new regional development strategy, a new economic development strategy and measures on employment equality. In relation to Targeting Social Need, a new initiative was agreed, together with a range of measures aimed at combating unemployment and progressively eliminating the differential in unemployment rates between the two communities by targeting objective need. Yet in all of this there was no explicit recognition of the widespread material inequalities both in Northern Ireland and the South, principally in relation to income and wealth. It appears that it was generally accepted that the neo-liberal economic paradigm could somehow produce the sustained economic growth necessary to eliminate poverty through full employment, together with a range of labour market-related measures, notwithstanding the evidence that the situation for large numbers of people in poverty could not be improved through these measures.[19] In addition, there was no recognition of the damage caused by the conflict to people's employment prospects because, for example, they were frightened to move out of their particular areas, their confidence, for one reason or another, was shattered, or they were debarred from particular types of work because of their criminal record. Anti-poverty measures, such as they were, were driven forward as if the conflict had never occurred.[20]

The Irish National Anti-Poverty Strategy (NAPS), launched in 1997, was explicitly framed in terms of the UN Copenhagen Summit discussed in Chapter 2.[21] Ireland was one of the few signatories (117 in all) to produce a follow-up plan fulfilling the commitment to produce 'time-bound goals and targets for the substantial reduction of overall poverty and the eradication of absolute poverty'.[22] The 1997 NAPS produced a precise definition and measures of poverty, as required under the UN agreement, and presented an analysis of poverty in terms of key social groups and problems.

One section of NAPS discusses the causes of poverty. It acknowledges that economic growth in the preceding decade mainly benefited those on higher incomes, but notes a slight fall in the proportion of the population in 'consistent' poverty (a measure which combines low income with basic deprivation). The principal cause of poverty was identified as unemployment and low pay, or the poor distribution of labour market participation across different groups, sectors and areas. Discrimination was identified as a particular problem in relation to women, people with disabilities and Travellers.

The NAPS has no specific reference to poverty and conflict. There is, however, an analysis of the issue in the background report for NAPS. This sees poverty and conflict as a two-way relationship:

> Not only is violence a major hindrance to addressing poverty and an important factor deepening poverty and social exclusion, but equally it must be acknowledged that poverty and social exclusion, while not a direct cause of violence can contribute to people's sense of alienation and exclusion and can be an important factor in the perpetuation of violence.[23]

The background report focuses mostly on the economic consequences of conflict rather than the kind of political effects of poverty which we have considered in Chapter 2. The conflict undermines economic growth, results in the diversion of resources away from dealing with social problems, distracts public attention from the issue of poverty, subverts respect for human rights and generally makes life worse for individuals and marginalised communities. Hence the main way forward – as seen one year prior to the 1998 Agreement – was to stop the conflict. Echoing the rhetoric of John Major's Government, the background report concluded: '[A]ny efforts to address poverty and social exclusion would be greatly enhanced by a permanent cease fire.'[24]

The NAPS discussion of conflict and poverty is pitched at a very general level. No attempt is made to identify specific issues, groups or localities that are conflict-related or in which the Irish government might have a particular interest. There is no mention of the distinctive nature of border areas for example. Nevertheless, the strategy does recognise that 'any long-term peace process must be reinforced by a clear strategy to address issues of poverty and social exclusion'.[25] There was some political support for this notion expressed in Dáil debates. One Deputy, for example, argued that:

> There is much evidence that societies emerging from conflict need huge input in a variety of areas if conflict resolution is to continue. Many resources will be needed to ensure this happens, North and South.[26]

A review of NAPS was published in February 2002. The updated NAPS is similar to the original plan in its focus on improving employment rates and the situation of older persons, children and young people, Travellers, those with disabilities, migrants and members of ethnic minorities, and women. It includes specific targets for eliminating long-term unemployment, raising benefit levels to €150 per week (2002 values, equivalent at the time to 30 per cent of gross average industrial earnings),[27] increasing educational participation,

163

reducing health inequalities and increasing the supply of housing, especially social housing. It is similar to the 1997 plan in that there are no actions in relation to poverty and conflict.

Unlike the South, Northern Ireland has never developed an explicit anti-poverty strategy. Measures aimed at poverty reduction derive from the UK government, including the National Action Plan on poverty and social exclusion, and apply to the whole of the UK and not specifically to Northern Ireland. As Conservative Governments were in power for all but six of the thirty years of the troubles, it is perhaps unsurprising that there has been no specific focus on poverty or inequality as they believed that a rising tide of prosperity would benefit everyone. When the Labour government came to power in 1997 it introduced a number of anti-poverty measures. The most politically significant commitment during its first term of office was to end child poverty in a generation and a specific commitment to reduce the child poverty rate by half in ten years. Other anti-poverty measures included a range of welfare-to-work programmes targeted at specific groups, a National Child Care Strategy, a minimum wage, major increases in child benefit and child-related allowances, a shift from benefits to tax credits and a range of new services with an explicit anti-poverty focus, such as Sure Start and Neighbourhood Renewal initiatives. However, there has been no commitment to reduce inequalities in income and wealth.

While there has been no explicit 'home grown' anti-poverty strategy in Northern Ireland until 2004 (see below), resources have been targeted at the most deprived areas through the use of area-based indicators, based initially on the Robson and then on the Noble Index. In 1991 the policy was made explicit in a programme called Targeting Social Need (TSN). This focused on tackling the most acute and serious problems of disadvantage. No extra resources were made available but the aim was to 'skew' existing resources towards areas scoring highest on measures of multiple disadvantage. This strategy was reviewed in 1998 and was relaunched with a number of changes as New TSN. Like the original TSN, New TSN involves no extra resources and is focused on 'unemployment and employability, tackling social need in other policy areas and promoting social inclusion'.[28] In April 2003 Deloitte and Touche published an interim evaluation of New TSN.[29] It noted that there was an absence of policy objectives and targets in relation to the three core strands of the policy – employability, unemployment and inequalities – which meant that individual departments made their own interpretations. The report itself did not define what it meant by these three terms, particularly 'inequalities'. However, it summarised their own assessment of the relevance of the New TSN to each of the eleven departments. Surprisingly, it considered that inequality was highly relevant to only four departments: Department of Education, Department of Employment and Learning, Department of Health, Social Services and Public Safety, and Department of Social Development. It clearly considered equality in terms of status rather than in terms of income and wealth, otherwise all departments would have been considered to be highly relevant.

Another criticism of New TSN is that it is largely discretionary and lacks any legal backing. As a result, Departments are able to go ahead with substantial investment strategies with little or no regard for targeting social need. There have been a number of projects in recent years that will produce little or no benefit for the most deprived sections of the community.[30]

In April 2004, the Office of First Minister and Deputy First Minister published *Towards an Anti-Poverty Strategy: New TSN – the Way Forward, A Consultation Document*. It is suggested that New TSN should evolve into a wider anti-poverty strategy and to this end it recommends a number of changes to the current policy. It suggests that a much greater emphasis be placed on outcomes and that progress should be measured against targets. The main recommendation is that 'the overall strategic objective of the Anti-Poverty strategy is to improve income and living conditions of the most disadvantaged'.[31]

The strategic framework, which the paper proposes for dealing with poverty, is based on policies similar to those that have proven inadequate in the past. First, it recommends 'building capacity' by which it means helping people to participate in the labour market and take advantage of the market economy. It makes no comment about the fact that jobs are still being lost in the manufacturing sector and that in many areas of Northern Ireland there simply are not enough jobs for everyone who wants one. At the same time, there are very real barriers to taking up jobs elsewhere. Second, the strategy involves increasing employment opportunities and reducing barriers to employment. These are the same policies that have been in place for many years, yet the numbers in poverty remain high. Third, the strategy proposes to prioritise financial hardship through increasing the uptake of financial entitlement and reducing indebtedness and financial hardship. While a useful initiative, it will have only a small impact on poverty levels. The poor are in debt because they do not have enough resources on which to live. The focus on financial hardship will have minimal effect on poverty levels.

This does not add up to a robust anti-poverty strategy for Northern Ireland. It is at best a strategy for economic growth and is likely to have only a marginal impact on the nature and extent of poverty. The paper does not provide a definition of the 'most disadvantaged' or a definition of poverty. It notes only that the 'range of definitions and measures poses specific challenges for research on poverty'.[32] It also poses a challenge for an anti-poverty strategy. There is no systematic analysis of the causes of poverty or the growing inequality in income and wealth in Northern Ireland. Nor is there any analysis of the way existing public expenditure could be redistributed towards the poor. And finally, there is no mention of the conflict and its relationship with poverty.

Another policy with potential impacts on poverty and its distribution was the commitment to promote equality of opportunity. Section 75 of the Northern Ireland Act 1998 places a duty on all public bodies to have due regard to the need to promote equality of opportunity between persons of different religious belief, political opinion, racial groups, age, marital status or sexual orientation, between men and women generally, between persons with a disability and persons without, and between persons with dependents and persons without.[33]

The major limitation of Section 75 is that it fails to include in the listed dimensions people from different social classes or with different financial circumstances. Following the legislation, considerable efforts have been made to assess the impact of new policies to ascertain whether they may disadvantage individuals across the nine dimensions, but there is no obligation to consider the impact on social class, one of the major divisions in Northern Ireland. As a result, widening class divisions are less visible and documented than unemployment by nominal religion.[34]

Turning to the EU, a strategy for eradicating poverty and social exclusion by the end of the decade was adopted in 2000. This involves each country submitting action plans to eliminate poverty and social exclusion (NAP/incl) every two years (starting 2001) and based on a common framework. For the first set of plans, countries used their own indicators, but for NAP/incl 2, ten primary and eight secondary indicators were agreed for all countries (the so-called Laeken indicators). It was open to countries to supplement these common indicators with third-level indicators dealing with national circumstances. The degree to which the EU framework has facilitated the integration of social and economic policy in the Irish case, including conflict, is debatable.[35]

The EU reporting structure does little to facilitate recognition of the specific importance of conflict and poverty. Ireland's recent experience of armed conflict is absent from the European Commission's first summary report based on each country's plan.[36] The EU Peace and Reconciliation Programme in Ireland and Northern Ireland is cited in the EU summary section as an example of an innovative approach to participation, alongside the UK Local Strategic Partnerships and the Alliance for Social Justice in the Netherlands. But why such a programme even exists is not alluded to. The UK report is entirely devoid of references to conflict or social division in Northern Ireland. The second report from the Irish government (for 2003–2005), however, contains the following statement:[37]

> The needs of disadvantaged communities are accentuated in the Border regions due to the effects of the conflict in Northern Ireland.[38]

As indicated, it is difficult to identify a border focus in Irish domestic anti-poverty policy. There is such a focus, however, in the 'common chapter' on North/South co-operation that appears in the National Development Plan (South) and the Northern Ireland Structural Funds Plan for 2000–2006. The common chapter states that:

> it is essential that the legacy of the troubles and violence of the past three decades is addressed so that the particular structural problems of the economy are tackled, community divisions and tensions are reduced, cross-community and north-south and east-west structures are developed and the problems of disadvantaged urban and rural areas are tackled on an effective and equitable basis.[39]

However, the degree to which the plan makes the link to poverty as such is minimal. One of the aims of the 'common chapter' is to identify areas where North/South co-operation has made a positive contribution to peace-building.[40] Evidently, co-operation on dealing with poverty is not included because much of the responsibility in this area is placed on existing policies, such as New TSN in Northern Ireland and NAPS in the South. These policies 'allow for appropriate priority to be given to such [border] disadvantaged areas and there is commitment to strengthen these policies'.[41] So, responsibility is channelled out of the 'common chapter' and back into policies that effectively ignore the issue of poverty and conflict.

The special EU programmes are examined in greater detail later on in this chapter. At this point, we underline that EU anti-poverty policy framework is not helping to highlight the general problem of poverty and conflict in Ireland, the specific problems associated with the border areas, and the situation of the peoples and areas most affected by the conflict in Northern Ireland. The nature of national reporting of plans for dealing with poverty and social exclusion is such that the distinctive problems in Northern Ireland get little attention. One reason for this is that income indicators for Northern Ireland have only recently become available. Another issue is the British government's centralist approach to poverty and social inclusion, notwithstanding devolution. This is partly because the policy levers that are key to any redistribution of income (taxes and welfare benefits) remain with the Treasury, but it also reflects a Northern Ireland civil service culture which for many years of direct rule looked to London for policy advice and prescription. At the basic level of social and economic data, comparisons between North and South, and between specific parts of Northern Ireland and the South, such as border areas, are still not readily and routinely available to inform the policy process.[42]

This suggests that 'national' reporting at EU level could be substantially improved in the case of Ireland by facilitating a 'common chapter' covering North and South, as well as developing border region comparisons. Priority could be given to conflict-related issues and to concerns that are self-evidently connected on a North/South basis, such as the labour market, welfare benefit levels, support for business development and inward investment, health, education, transport and the environment.

Social and political reconstruction in Ireland: an audit

The international evidence suggests the need for social and political reconstruction, as well as economic and physical reconstruction. The elements of this include human rights, dealing with the past, demobilisation and demilitarisation, the involvement of women, children and young people, as well as funding for peace. This section looks at each of these in turn and assesses the extent to which each has been present in Ireland, North and South.

Human rights

The 1998 Agreement committed the British and Irish governments to incorporating the European Convention on Human Rights into the legal systems of Northern Ireland and the Republic, and establishing equivalent Human Rights Commissions North and South, the first in Western Europe.[43]

Valuable as these developments have been, not least at the symbolic level, they fall short of the full-blooded commitment to human rights urged by the international community in relation to conflict transformation of war-torn societies. Guaranteeing a culture of human rights for the future in a society where such a culture has been absent or depleted previously requires firstly, reforming those institutions whose reputation was particularly tarnished in the past and secondly, dealing with the human rights abuses of the past. As in other societies, these were highly contentious in the Irish situation. Yet, as other societies have shown, where there is a fundamental commitment to human rights, developments are possible, even against the odds. The reform of policing and criminal justice institutions whose past reputation was controversial from a human rights perspective is now considered.

Policing

Policing is clearly contentious in the post-conflict situation in Northern Ireland.[44] This is because of the continuation of a number of debates about policing issues from the period of conflict. Such issues include: the sectarian make-up of the Royal Ulster Constabulary (88 percent Protestant), its role in shoot-to-kill operations, its use of plastic bullets with fatal consequences, serious allegations of collusion with loyalist paramilitary groups, and the impunity of the Special Branch. Because of these debates, the 1998 Agreement provided for the setting up of an Independent Commission on Policing for Northern Ireland, with a very clear mandate:

> The participants [in the negotiations] believe it essential that policing structures and arrangements are such that the police service is professional, effective and efficient, fair and impartial, free from partisan political control; accountable, both under the law for its actions and to the community it serves; representative of the society it polices, and operates within a coherent and co-operative criminal justice system, which conforms with human rights norms.[45]

The Patten Commission (called after its chairperson, Chris Patten) produced a radical report making nearly 300 recommendations.[46] It recommended a transformation in policing, introducing a multi-agency system in which policing is a function of the state, private organisations and local communities. However, key recommendations were either ignored or introduced in a highly restrictive manner.

Underlying the whole report was a fundamental premise, namely that the police should not be the sole supplier of policing. Policing must involve a whole 'network of intersecting regulatory mechanisms' in which policing becomes 'everybody's business'. The government, on this model, operates indirectly, seeking the participation of non-state agencies, private organisations and individuals and devolves responsibility for crime and security to them. The underlying premise is that it is impossible for a state to provide security for everyone. In such a model, the police become one of many 'nodes' of policing – not the sole node – and the task of the Policing Board is to regulate and support all the various policing activities. Thus if a local community wishes to have wardens to deal with anti-social youth in the area, it could apply to the Policing Board for a grant to carry out this policing function. Part of the thinking behind this radical conceptualisation of policing was the need to break the current monopoly of policing, which is held by the police. Only through establishing alternatives to the police, it is suggested, would they become more receptive to the needs of the community. Thus, instead of the police telling the communities and other organisations what they should do, the police would have to listen and respond to ideas from the grass roots.

This fundamental aspect of the Patten Commission was ignored in all the subsequent debates over emblems, affirmative action and other contentious recommendations. Moreover, the key to the success of such a strategy – that extra finances could be raised from the rates for a wide range of policing initiatives – was not accepted by the government.

While the Royal Ulster Constabulary has now been replaced by the Police Service of Northern Ireland (PSNI), policing remains the exclusive responsibility of the police. Moreover, the Policing Board, as established, is almost exclusively concerned with the financing and accountability of the police rather than being a 'police' board. There is no available evidence that it has attempted to broaden its remit in line with Pattern and support a wide range of grass-roots policing initiatives. While the Patten recommendation that District Policing Partnerships (DPP) should be established has been accepted, their powers are limited. At public meetings the police report on their efforts to reduce crime but note that they have limited resources to meet the demands. In turn the DPP reports on the numerous complaints it has received from the local community about the level of crime. The solution for both is seen as more resources for the police.

The cost of policing already amounts to over £700 million a year. If this is added to the cost of the criminal justice and prison system the total spent on 'the law and order' function constitutes one-tenth of the total public expenditure in Northern Ireland. This issue rarely, if ever, becomes part of the public debate. Nor indeed has there been any serious debate of the failure to deal with the concern expressed two decades ago by John Stalker, that the Special Branch was a force within a force.[47] The Special Branch and the Criminal Investigation Division are under a unified command since June 2004, but how this affects the autonomy of the Special Branch remains to be seen.

Criminal justice reform

The 1998 Agreement also provides for a 'wide-ranging review of criminal justice (other than policing and those aspects of the system relating to the emergency legislation)...'[48] However, it is impossible to understand the operations of the criminal justice system over the last three decades in Ireland, North and South, without examining the effects of emergency legislation on the system overall. In the South, special courts, military tribunals and emergency legislation have taken political offenders out of the regular criminal justice system into a special system. In Northern Ireland there has been the establishment of non-jury courts (Diplock courts) to try what are known as scheduled (i.e. politically motivated) offences, emergency legislation such as the Prevention of Terrorism Act and the Emergency Provisions Act, and, during the 1970s, special category status for politically motivated prisoners. Critics point to numerous ways in which the operation of the criminal justice system has been affected by these developments, not least in relation to the 'case hardening'[49] of judges sitting without the benefit of a jury, which has been noted from an early stage in the existence of the Diplock Courts.[50]

The review of criminal justice made 294 recommendations, the most important of which related to the establishment of a Judicial Appointments Commission and Community Safety and Policing Partnerships chaired by local authority members.[51] In November 2001 the Government published an implementation plan followed by the Justice (Northern Ireland) Act 2002. However, few of the recommendations were covered in the Act and the Joint Declaration of the British and Irish governments of April 2003 noted a number of measures to ensure implementation of the recommendations of the Criminal Justice Review. The government has now published a new Justice (NI) Bill which was due to become law in 2004.

None of the recommendations of the review was costed. The suggested reforms are likely to come to many millions of pounds, yet there has been no debate as to whether this is the most appropriate way to spend public resources. Meanwhile, expenditure on the criminal justice system continues to expand rapidly. A key element of the Court Service's future plans is to modernise court buildings, and nearly £6 million is committed to this over the next two years.[52] The flagship of the Court Service is the Laganside Court complex, which was financed through a Private Finance Initiative scheme. The cost of the project, which included mothballing the old Crumlin Road Courts, was £40 million.[53] The annual rent is £2.5 million and will total £61 million over the 25 years.[54]

While the working environments of the legal profession are being upgraded, thousands of children throughout Northern Ireland are being educated in decaying and crumbling school buildings, which require £750 million just to deal with highest priority categories.[55] Though £500 million has been spent on schools in the last two years, it is not enough to address the crisis of crumbling school buildings. The challenge is how to reprioritise expenditure from criminal justice to issues around social justice.

Dealing with the past

When violent political conflicts end there is frequently a move to uncover the truth about past human rights abuses, often formalised in a truth commission.[56] The move towards formal truth-seeking mechanisms in relation to Northern Ireland has been tentative. Despite arguments in favour of truth-seeking soon after the 1994 cease-fires,[57] there has been little agreement about the need for, and nature and timing of any formal truth process.

The establishment of a truth commission was not raised at any point during the talks which led to the 1998 Agreement. Instead, to balance the concerns of unionists in relation to the early release of politically motivated prisoners, much was made in the Agreement of the need to 'acknowledge and address the suffering of the victims of violence as a necessary element of reconciliation'.[58] Shortly after the signing of the 1998 Agreement, the Bloomfield report on policies relating to victims was published. The report concluded that: 'The possibility of benefiting from some form of Truth and Reconciliation Commission at some stage should not be overlooked',[59] but showed no urgency in taking the debate further. The report from the Victims Commission in the Republic of Ireland was equally non-committal.[60]

From time to time there has been somewhat muted support for the idea of a truth commission from other sources.[61] Those involved in the *All Truth is Bitter* report[62] stressed the need for 'an agreed truth as a vital means of moving on from conflict', while at the same time urging caution about a truth and reconciliation commission as the best means of reaching such an agreement. The Healing through Remembering Project,[63] although more detailed on the potential advantages of and obstacles to a truth recovery process, in the end could not go beyond the divergent opinions of those it had consulted. Similarly, the Northern Ireland Human Rights Commission[64] has firmly acknowledged that there is a right to truth when conflicts end but does not suggest any detailed blueprint for a truth-recovery process for Northern Ireland. It has been left to groups within the broader nationalist and civil liberties community to keep debate about a truth commission, such as experienced in other post-conflict societies, alive. One such group, Eolas, has gone as far as producing a number of possible blueprints which could be considered if a truth commission is to be tried.[65]

Up to this point the British government had been studiously silent in response to calls from republican and other groups for consideration to be given to a formal truth recovery process. The public nature of the debate moved up a step in February 2004 when chair of the Policing Board, Des Rea,[66] and Chief Constable Hugh Orde both suggested, in quick succession, the possibility of a truth commission. This was prompted by the Chief Constable's expressed concern about an endless stream of demands for public inquiries (such as that into the murder in 1989 of solicitor Pat Finucane).[67] In June 2004, Secretary of State Paul Murphy travelled to South Africa in order to examine the relevance of its Truth and Reconciliation Commission to Northern Ireland. He stated that a truth commission for Northern Ireland would take the form of 'a forum for story-telling'.[68]

The proposed story-telling approach would not involve investigation of previous practices of the state and its institutions, as well as other institutions in society. For example, while the story-telling aspect of South Africa's Truth and Reconciliation Commission is well known, less well publicised, at least internationally, were its institutional hearings into the role of institutions, such as the media, business and the churches, in the apartheid regime. The Commission found that:

> Business was central to the economy that sustained the South African state during the apartheid years. Certain businesses, especially the mining industry, were involved in helping to design and implement apartheid policies. Other businesses benefited from co-operating with the

security structures of the former state. Most businesses benefited from operating in a racially structured context.[69]

There is scope for such projects in Ireland. The 2002 *Northern Ireland Life and Times Survey* revealed that 86 per cent of people surveyed (89 per cent of Catholics, 82 percent of Protestants and 92 percent of those with no religion) said that they would prefer to work in mixed workplaces.[70] Yet there is little evidence of the business community, and in particular the large scale transnational companies, seeking to prioritise the provision of such workplaces. It can be argued that to leave this development to the workings of fair employment legislation, no matter how robust, or the activities of the Equality Commission is insufficient. To live up to the ideal, companies would need to be making independent and proactive efforts to guarantee diversity.

Demobilisation and demilitarisation

In Chapter 3 we noted the importance of successful demobilisation of combatants in the process of conflict transformation. Successful demobilisation makes a major contribution to a smooth demilitarisation of society. In turn, the wisdom of international practice is that the most successful demobilisation occurs when the ex-combatants themselves are in charge of the process, utilising a community development approach.

There have been mixed messages in terms of demilitarisation in the Irish context. The number of British troops in Northern Ireland has been cut back, but the current level of 12,000 troops is still much greater than the peacetime garrison figure of 5,000. Similarly, while five British Army observation towers in South Armagh have been dismantled since 2000, eight still remain.[71] In the same vein, the Patten Report recommended cutting the number of police officers by 6,000 to a level of 7,500 over a ten-year period. This move, although having the backing of the Chief Constable, is being resisted by sections of the PSNI. Such a reduction in personnel would seem to guarantee a large reduction in the police budget. Yet, according to the Northern Ireland Office Departmental Report for 2003, overall policing and security costs were £604 million for the financial year in which the Agreement was signed (1998/1999). That figure rose to £812 million in 2001/2002 and is projected to be £831 million by 2005/2006.[72]

One factor contributing to continued high spending levels is the cost of severance pay for police personnel. The budget for this item comes to £240 million up to 2005/2006, most of the cost falling in the 2001–2003 period. The rising level of policing expenditure cannot be explained by severance costs however. Excluding severance, the police and security budget will have increased by a third over the seven years 1998/1999 to 2005/2006.[73] This is quite the reverse of what might be expected, even in post-war societies that maintain high levels of security spending.

The Annual Reports of An Garda Síochána show that the police budget in the South increased by about 20 per cent from 1999 to 2002.[74] Similarly, the cost of the British Army shows no sign of falling back to pre-conflict levels. In fact, figures for the number of British Army personnel stationed in Northern Ireland reveal a larger fall before the 1998 Agreement than after it.[75]

Army costs increased by 7 per cent from 1995/1996 to 1997/1998.[76] In the Agreement year, 1998, the Ministry of Defence revealed that it had spent £21.4 million of capital provision for the armed forces in Northern Ireland in the previous 12 months and planned a further £54.7 million on maintenance and development in the following year.[77]

An argument for maintaining high police expenditure is that armed groups continue to exist and are still engaged in fund-raising activities, and are even expanding their activities. There is the view that the well-armed 'terrorist godfathers' have made career moves into mainstream gangsterism and organised crime. This scenario is increasingly used to justify criminal justice budgets, powers and activities in both jurisdictions in Ireland. As one Deputy put it 'we are now experiencing a peace dividend. Places are now available in the high security prison in Portlaoise for serious criminals and drug barons which were previously held exclusively for subversives'.[78]

Another example is the report prepared by the Northern Ireland Affairs Committee on *The Financing of Terrorism in Northern Ireland*.[79] The report is particularly concerned about money laundering, fuel and tobacco smuggling, business and social security fraud, and counterfeiting. The evidential basis for the threat posed by such activities is not strong. PSNI estimates submitted to the Committee suggested that republican groups needed about £2 million a year to function and loyalists between £1.8 and £2.8 million. The 'fundraising capacity' of republicans, however, was said to be between £10 and £13 million per year, whereas loyalists can manage between £4 and £4.5 million.[80]

The report concludes that 'organised crime, whether or not it is directly linked to terrorism, *has the potential to* corrupt and undermine the economy by distorting markets and making normal business practice impossible.' (emphasis added)[81]

This vagueness is matched by the parliamentary answers given by Ministers to questions about the activities of the Organised Crime Task Force. This was set up in 2000 and is made up of the Northern Ireland Office, PSNI, HM Customs and Excise, Inland Revenue, Northern Ireland Court Service, Home Office, Assets Recovery Bureau and a number of unspecified 'other government agencies'. It publishes annual Threat Assessments. In its 2003 report it noted that some 700 individuals were involved in organised crime networks in Northern Ireland and that paramilitaries were involved in two-thirds of the crime groups identified. It also believed that 'paramilitary groups were increasingly turning to organised crime'.[82] That there is paramilitary involvement in different forms of crime is beyond doubt, but the lack of arrests or seizure of assets suggests that the scale and extent of this activity may be exaggerated.

Overall, there is too much emphasis on an ill-defined problem of 'organised crime' to the detriment of other issues, and a subsequent failure to acknowledge that 'organised crime' has a variety of different origins and takes different forms in the two communities in Northern Ireland. Some crimes are rooted in social and economic deprivation of specific areas in which there are no jobs and 'entrepreneurial' members of these communities turn to illegal activities to provide income for themselves and their families. Other types of crimes have their origins in the conflict itself and were developed to provide resources for armed groups on both sides. It would be surprising if all of this activity stopped with the signing of the 1998 Agreement unless there were alternative forms of income for those involved. Other criminal activity owes its origin directly to the behaviour of the security services. It is now well documented that numerous informers were recruited by the police and other security organisations and a blind eye was turned to their criminal behaviour, further expanding the level of illegality in both communities.[83] Given these very different origins, the level of paramilitary activities is unlikely to be radically reduced by an organised task force, political vetting of voluntary organisations (as recommended by the IMC) or by a criminal justice response.

One issue that has been grossly overlooked is the success of groups working with demobilised ex-prisoners. For example, Coiste na n-Iarchímí, a group working with republican ex-combatants, employs a self-help and community development logic. They have organised training, counselling, education and employment schemes, thus enabling large numbers of ex-prisoners to recognise that they have a stake in society and a role to play in building a future different from the past.[84] To a lesser extent, loyalist ex-prisoners' groups, such as the Ex-Prisoners Interpretative Centre (EPIC), have followed the same route. Arguably, the role of ex-combatants in Ireland in demobilising themselves with a minimum of official support provides one of the best examples globally of successful demobilisation.

The successes of organisations such as Coiste are all the more significant given the miniscule financial support they have been given. While funding for the PNSI is constantly increased, 61 groups working with politically motivated ex-prisoners received only £5.12 million from Peace I between 1995 and 1999. The follow-up programme, Peace II, allowed for work on reintegration of victims, but made little provision for ex-prisoners. The Programme for Government of the devolved Northern Ireland Assembly has no mention of the need to help reintegrate politically motivated ex-prisoners.[85]

Women

Rising levels of gender-based violence against women are occurring in Northern Ireland.[86] Although they have not reached the horrific scale of rape in post-apartheid South Africa, they pose worrying questions for the construction of a post-conflict society. One dimension of this is the warrior-type of masculinity evident in paramilitary organisations and security forces in a society which Cathy Harkin of Derry Women's Aid once typified as an 'armed patriarchy'.[87] There are 134,000 legally held small arms in Northern Ireland. One person in eighteen holds a shotgun certificate compared with half that ratio in England and Wales. This proliferation of firearms, a direct result of conflict, has been a significant factor in the nature of domestic violence. McWilliams and McKeirnan show the inadequacy of the criminal justice system to respond and protect the partners of certain firearms certificate holders – particularly those in the security forces – from the most violent control and abuse.[88]

Similarly, in conflict situations elsewhere, women may have assumed economic roles that were previously closed, as a consequence of the imprisonment or death of adult males. In Northern Ireland, the wives of long-term prisoners often found themselves in a 'head of household' situation that they came to value, but which caused difficulties with male partners on release.[89]

These important issues apart, the central question regarding gendering reconstruction in Northern Ireland relates to the extent to which the 1998 Agreement has delivered on its pledge to afford 'full and equal participation of women in public life'. The record is not good: notwithstanding assertions to the contrary,[90] governments, politicians and elements of civil society seem to be content to see women confined to working on cross-community 'bread and butter' issues, leaving the 'real work' to men. Women have remained largely excluded from participation in institutions that are most directly concerned with conflict prevention, like the Parades Commission and the higher echelons of the criminal justice system, as well as the senior levels of most political parties.[91] There remains a significant gap between a political commitment to the inclusion of women and practice on the ground. A commitment to 'gendering reconstruction', evident in transitional societies elsewhere, is remarkably absent in the Irish situation.

The Irish National Report to the UN General Assembly, regarding the implementation of Beijing obligations, makes reference to a government policy of 40 per cent representation of both genders on state boards. While this had raised the overall percentage to 27 per cent women, the lack of any mandatory commitment to quotas has meant that it is unlikely that parity will be achieved in the foreseeable future.[92] Meanwhile, the Irish government's draft National Plan for Women (2001–2005) stated that its commitments regarding women and armed conflict include consideration of a 'level of support to women's organisations in Ireland working for peace and development in Ireland and abroad.'[93]

Community-based women's groups have developed throughout Ireland in the past two decades, in response to women's needs for education and advice. It is estimated that there are at least 1,000 women's education groups on the whole of the island, each catering for between 50 and 500 women annually.[94] In the South, the National Women's Council of Ireland lists 2,631 organisations catering for about 75,000 women.[95] Research figures from Northern Ireland in 2001 estimated 1,071 'traditional' groups and 423 'activist' women's organisations, with 68 per cent of organisations located in areas defined as economically deprived.[96] The importance of women's self-help and political benefits from such organisations are attested to in all areas where there has been civil conflict:

> Often women meet to discuss issues they find of concern in their society, but also because they want to empower themselves and others. Forming or becoming a member of an organisation can be a way for women to heal their war traumas. Sharing painful memories makes it easier to lessen feelings of hatred and start to think of the future. Becoming involved in an organisation is also a good stepping stone into politics. Discussing problems and possible solutions helps women become better equipped for making proposals for changes within society.[97]

A practical demonstration of such benefits can be seen in the cultural exchange programme involving women from both sides of the border that was developed by Women Educating for Transformation (WEFT). Three cross-border partnerships, each involving two women's cross-community groups, met over a thirty-week period, their dialogue structured around the recognition that 'women's experience of the conflict in Northern Ireland and the social, political and cultural divisions that resulted from this, compounded the general injustice and disadvantage experienced by women in society.'[98] The experiences of development and growth achieved by participants were summed up as follows:

> Examples of empowerment included, experiencing being valued for themselves and for their differences, understanding themselves in a wider historical

framework, beginning to resolve feelings of separation and alienation from the troubled North, taking active ownership of the Good Friday Agreement, and wishing to be involved in the making of a new dispensation in Ireland North and South, through participation at community and national level.[99]

The Southern border region in Ireland has suffered considerably as a consequence of partition, and community development work is an essential aspect of the overall task of reconstruction. The analysis of the economic, social/cultural and political disadvantages of the border counties presented by McMinn and O'Meara in their IFI-funded research into the sustainability of community women's groups in the six Southern border counties highlights the importance of the work undertaken by the women's community sector in that region, as a 'life changing force for women, both individually and for their communities'.[100] Economic participation rates for women are below the national average, while educational levels are lower than normal. More than two hundred women's groups exist in the area, although there are only 30–35 full-time workers, mostly funded by ADM/CPA through the Peace Programme. The rest of the work is largely voluntary, a situation that does not allow for sustainable development in the sector. At the same time, the level of disadvantage experienced by women in the border regions is such that their disempowerment hinders their ability to participate fully in reconstruction.

In Northern Ireland, over forty community-based women's centres, women's projects and women's infrastructure groups are affiliated to the Women's Support Network (WSN), established in 1989 as an umbrella organisation to provide information, support and lobbying expertise in the promotion of the autonomous organisation of women. Thirty-five per cent of women's groups are in the Belfast District Council area, the majority located within areas defined as deprived according to the Northern Ireland Multiple Deprivation Measure (Noble Index) where they 'are invariably at the heart of community development initiatives within their communities'.[101] Taillon's research has indicated the invaluable services provided by this women's sector, ranging from welfare advice, health and well-being services, policy development, education classes, childcare, and their importance in sustaining communities fractured by conflict and social and economic deprivation.[102] In a survey of the experiences of women's organisations in accessing EU funding and the importance of their work in combating the social exclusion of economically disadvantaged women, lone parents, elderly and young women, women with disabilities, ethnic minorities and Traveller women, and ex-prisoners and their families, exclusion was evident.[103]

The advocacy and campaigning work undertaken by women's groups has extended far beyond their initial preoccupations with exclusively women's issues. While women's groups have been the catalyst for general community development in some areas, their ability to develop social capital remains constrained by the nature of the relationship between the women's sector and the wider community. In many areas that have experienced acute inter-communal violence, the ability of female activists to provide positive examples of acts rooted in a desire to promote reconciliation is limited because of the dominance of male community leaders following different agendas. In different ways the testimonies of the women's centres collated by Taillon provide evidence that such attitudes remain, as reflected in the report of Windsor Women's Centre:

> ... we are continuing with our efforts to ensure that women's views and experiences are listened to and valued by the government agencies who are working within this community. Our experience has been while women are the mainstream of everyday community work when it comes to the perceived 'big' issues they are often marginalised and not given an equal place in decision making.[104]

Yet there is a crisis in Ireland in terms of the long-term sustainability of the women's community sector. Their activities, which expanded considerably with the advent of EU peace money, are now under threat as this financial underpinning comes to an end. The evidence amassed by the Women's Support Network demonstrates that women's organisations have, over the years, been forced to depend on an ever-narrowing range of funding sources. In the years 1997–2000, more than half of all funding to Belfast Women's Centres came from EU programmes or the National Lottery (later the Community Fund). Mainstreaming some of the services provided by community-based women's organisations could help to secure longer-term funding and increase the influence of women's groups, but it might also 'entail changes in procedures and forms of accountability which some women would view as counter to the ethos of women's community work'.[105] It could also mean the eventual marginalisation of women activists.[106] The precarious nature of community-based women's organisations must be redressed but this will only be achieved when there is real recognition of the overall importance of the work of the sector.

Children and young people

Des Browne, former Northern Ireland Office minister, once asked why the rights of children in Newcastle, County Down, should be different from those in Newcastle, England. In one sense, there should be no difference. But children and young people in Northern Ireland do need special consideration in terms of guaranteeing rights. Five hundred and fifty-seven people under the age of 20 were killed during the conflict.[107] Seven of the 16 deaths caused by rubber and plastic bullets were of children under the age of 18.[108] One survey found that 32 per cent of children aged between 14 and 17 had witnessed someone being killed or seriously injured during the conflict.[109] Add to that the fact that Northern Ireland has significantly higher levels of children living in poverty than any other region of the UK,[110] and that infant mortality rates for children of the Travelling community are three times that of the general population, and it is clear that children in Northern Ireland face a range of specific issues. Children have been further affected as refugees, exiles for anti-social behaviour or victims of punishment beatings.

Despite this, the situation of children and young people was not directly addressed in the 1998 Agreement. Since 1998, as indeed before, the Children's Law Centre and other organisations in Northern Ireland have been active on behalf of recognising the specific needs of children and young people in a post-conflict society.[111] Their efforts have led to the appointment of a Children's Commissioner for Northern Ireland and they continue to argue for the recognition of the specific needs of children and young people in the proposed Bill of Rights.[112]

The Children's Commissioner's role is restricted by the requirement that the incumbent must work within the existing legal framework of rights provisions for children and young people. In addressing the needs of children, given that the Bill of Rights does not yet exist, the UN Convention on the Rights of the Child has not been incorporated into domestic law, and Section 75 of the Northern Ireland Act 1998 does not acknowledge the specific rights of children and young people, there is clearly some distance yet to go.

In the South there is a National Children's Strategy, a National Children's Office and an Ombudsman for Children. These developments have been driven forward by the UN Convention on the Rights of the Child rather than by any direct focus on the damage inflicted on children and young people by violent conflict on the island of Ireland.

The Criminal Justice Review in Northern Ireland recommended the establishment of community restorative justice schemes for juvenile offenders.[113] This was implemented as a result of the Justice (NI) Act 2002. Consequently, there is a range of imaginative innovations taking place which ensure that the approach to children and young people is taken somewhat out of the criminal justice system. For example, the PSNI now has a Youth Diversion Scheme which seeks to use restorative justice approaches to young offenders or those at risk of offending or becoming involved in anti-social behaviour.[114] These advances are currently under threat as a result of the NIO's introduction of Anti-Social Behaviour Orders (ASBOs). The experience to date in England and Wales is that ASBOs have been used mainly against children and young people, rather than adults, frequently for 'offences' such as 'hanging around'. Ironically, given moves to take children and young people out of the criminal justice system, breach of an ASBO is a criminal offence, with a maximum sentence of five years imprisonment.

Funding peace in Ireland

Reconstruction in other war-torn societies has involved, often for the first time, international bodies – governments and NGOs – in funding and indeed guiding conflict transformation. In the Irish case, as we saw earlier, a preliminary move in this direction was signalled by the establishment by the British and Irish governments of the International Fund for Ireland in 1985 in the aftermath of the Anglo-Irish Agreement.

A similar, but larger, intervention occurred in 1995 in the aftermath of the cease-fires. The EU established a special programme for Northern Ireland and the six border counties, which became known as Peace I. When this programme expired in 2000, it was replaced by Peace II, a mainstream EU programme under the European Structural Funds. The significance of the shift from a special programme to a mainstream programme will become apparent shortly.

A vibrant community sector developed during the conflict in Northern Ireland, not least because of the need for communities to help themselves in the absence of support from outside, including from the state. Peace I dovetailed neatly with many of the priorities and principles of this community sector and in doing so came close to matching some of the ideals of global conflict transformation. As we identified in Chapter 3, such ideals include:

- political engagement – working *on* conflict and not just *around* or *in* conflict;

- direct support for civil society – supporting projects that grow from the grass roots;

- prioritising a community development approach rather than merely service delivery.

Peace I prioritised social inclusion, 'a process which sought to address the needs of excluded or vulnerable groups and which identified routes or pathways to ensure integration-re-integration into social, economic, political and cultural activity'.[115] In doing so, it not only supported the voluntary and community movement, but also proactively sought out areas where community infrastructure was weak and built capacity there, not least in unionist/loyalist areas.[116] This approach required a great deal of flexibility: 'Measures could, and often did, build capacity and confidence and move people on to peace building activities outside their own community or interest group. But there were no easily measurable outcomes ...'[117] Because it was outside mainstream EU structures, groups were allowed to take risks for social inclusion and peace-building. As a result, the consensus of the community and voluntary sector was that Peace I was successful in relation to achieving its four main goals: it developed grass-roots capacities and promoted the inclusion of women; it promoted the inclusion of vulnerable and marginalised groups; it provided programmes for victims and ex-prisoners; and it encouraged cross-border reconciliation.[118]

Ideally, these positive lessons of Peace I should have informed the design and delivery of Peace II, which began in 2000. And in one sense they did. Many commentators had argued that Peace I had been remarkably imprecise in terms of defining peace and reconciliation. The architects of Peace II took this criticism seriously and focused the programme on peace-building through the application of 'distinctiveness' criteria. To be eligible for Peace funding, groups had to 'address the legacy of the conflict' or take 'opportunties for peace-building' and 'pave the way to reconciliation'. Addressing issues of deprivation or social inclusion per se was no longer sufficient basis for funding. The effect of this was to make it more difficult for a number of community and voluntary groups to fit the criteria of Peace II. '... people faced with some of the severest social exclusion problems suffered from the diminished emphasis on the social inclusion objective. Unlike victims of the Troubles or politically-motivated ex-prisoners, it was more difficult for the victims of social-economic exclusion to fulfil the peacebuilding requirement ...'[119] This shortcoming of Peace II is particularly evident in border areas. In addition, the decision was taken that the new programme was to have a much stronger emphasis on economic development. Being a part of the Structural Funds also meant a very strong emphasis on bureaucracy and accounting, which made it difficult for small groups to access funds. As a result of these decisions, Peace II is less able to develop the linkages between peace and poverty, which are at the core of this report.

As a result, Peace II failed in significant ways to learn the lessons of Peace I. To take one important example: at an early stage a new measure was suggested for Peace II, one which had not existed in Peace I, 'Outward and forward looking region'. The objective of this measure was 'to link NI and the Republic to the wider world of conflict resolution',[120] in essence an innovative opportunity to make the kind of connections we have been making throughout this report. But when Peace II was established, the budget for this measure had been cut from €27m to €11m, the Republic was excluded from the measure and most of money was allocated to the Northern Ireland Tourist Board!

At times in the past, for the nationalist community in particular, community development took place not merely in the absence of state support but also in the face of state obstruction. Thus Northern Ireland has had its experience of conditionality – financial support dependent on external demands on behaviour – most obviously when community groups were starved of state funding if, in the words of then Secretary of State for Northern Ireland Douglas Hurd, it was suspected they had 'sufficiently close links with paramilitary organisations to give rise to a grave risk that to give support to those groups would have the effect of improving the standing and furthering the aims of a paramilitary organisation, whether directly or indirectly'.[121] This crude approach is in danger of being repeated in the near future following the report of the Independent Monitoring Commission.[122]

Conclusion: A lost opportunity

This chapter reviewed a range of lost opportunities to strengthen the Irish peace process – anti-poverty and inequality measures, human rights, justice, truth, policing, the needs of ex-combatants, women, children and young people. These are the issues and groups of people who have been at the forefront of reconstruction programmes in other societies coming out of conflict. This is not to say that the programmes have always delivered; but the difference in the Irish case is that in many ways reconstruction has not been tried, or only to a limited extent.

In a number of crucial ways Peace I came close to incorporating an element of reconstruction. It was underwritten by a number of principles that would be familiar to international NGOs involved in reconstruction in other parts of the world: bypassing state structures to fund the grass roots; supporting community development initiatives; flexibility in relation to accountancy and management to allow for innovation; prioritising the demobilisation of ex-combatants. But Peace I was a special programme that broke the normal rules of EU funding. It was perhaps inevitable that it would be replaced by Peace II, a mainstream programme that followed the more familiar bureaucratic rules of such programmes and was not unlike previous European Social Fund and European Regional Development Fund measures. Harvey, who researched the origins of Peace II intensively, notes the differences in personnel in the planning and design of both programmes:

> The new programme was heavily influenced by the new Northern Ireland Executive ... At the administrative level, many of the key Commission officials most influential in the Peace I programme had moved on to new positions. This marked a dramatic difference from Peace I, where the programme texts were drafted and amended in Brussels. This time, the creative thinking of the Commission was almost absent.[123]

But there was more than that involved: in the absence of ongoing structures to intervene in post-conflict Ireland, the default was to design programmes according to standard EU conventions. There were winners and losers in this process, the winners being economic development, elected representatives, and local authorities, while the losers were social inclusion, and the voluntary and community sector.[124]

Yet, plausible as this explanation may appear, there is one flaw in the argument. As we have seen in Chapter 3, the EU has tried and trusted mechanisms to intervene in post-conflict societies. The involvement of the European Agency for Reconstruction (EAR) in places such as the Balkans, East Timor and South Africa is characterised by emphases on civil society, democracy and human rights and not merely on economic or physical reconstruction. And the European Parliament sees the work of the EAR as a model to be used in reconstructing other transitional societies such as Afghanistan.

The difference in the case of Ireland is obvious; the Balkans, East Timor, South Africa, Afghanistan are all outside the EU, while Ireland is a member country. Authors such as Belloni,[125] Moore[126] and Stiefel[127] have concluded that the West's intervention in the reconstruction of war-torn societies is imbued with neo-colonial prejudice. Conversely, Ireland is seen as a normal, democratic society within the EU, albeit one with severe ethno-nationalist[128] problems. In that sense, Ireland is not special and does not need a special programme.

Reconstruction is for failed or failing states and there was no appetite in official EU quarters to include a member state within that rubric. To do so would be to side with the analysis of one of the insurgent forces within the Irish conflict and to be contrary to the view of the Irish government. Most of all, it would have challenged three decades of British policy in Northern Ireland, where 'normalisation' was central.

To go beyond 'normalisation' to 'reconstruction' would have meant overcoming denial in order to seek the political roots of conflict and poverty. If the Irish conflict did not result from crime or atavism, then what was the role of colonialism, partition, discrimination, repression? This was a Pandora's box which was not easily opened.

1   Morrissey, M. and Gaffikin, F. (1990) *Northern Ireland: the Thatcher Years*, London: Zed.

2   http://www.eu2004.ie/templates/standard.asp?sNavlocator=7,93,180

3   Sheehan, M. (1995) *The International Fund for Ireland: Some Findings on its Patterns of Expenditure*, Belfast: West Belfast Economic Forum.

4   Rolston, B. and Tomlinson, M. (1988) *Unemployment in West Belfast: the Obair Report*, Belfast: Beyond the Pale Publications.

5   The European Court of Auditors expressed 'concern about the doubtful "additionality" of some of the expenditure' of IFI. See Special Report No. 7/2000 concerning the International Fund for Ireland and the Special Support Programme for Peace and Reconciliation in Northern Ireland and the Border Counties of Ireland.
    http://www.publications.parliament.uk/pa/cm199900/cmselect/cmeule g/23-xx/2315.htm

6   *The Irish Catholic*, Thursday, May 27 2004, p 11.

7   *The Guardian*, 29 January 2004.

8   Cragin, K. and Chalk, P. (2003) *Terrorism and Development: Using Social and Economic Development to Inhibit a Resurgence of Terrorism*, Santa Monica, CA: Rand Corporation, p. 11.

9   John McKinney, Chief Executive of the Special EU Programmes body, the managing authority for Peace II.
    http://www.nirailways.co.uk/20030128newbuses.asp

10 Barringon, K. (2004) 'Threat to economy from North deal', *Sunday Business Post*, 28 November.

11 See Morrissey, M. (2000) 'Northern Ireland: Developing a post-conflict economy', in M. Cox, A. Guelke and F. Stephen (eds.) *A Farewell to Arms? From 'long war' to long peace in Northern Ireland*, Manchester: Manchester University Press, pp. 136–152; also, *Building on Peace: Supporting Peace and Reconciliation after 2006*, Monaghan/Dublin: ADM/CPA. pp. 80–97.

12 Mac Ginty, R. and Darby, J. (2002) *Guns and Government: The Management of the Northern Ireland Peace Process*, Basingstoke: Palgrave. p. 136.

13 Wilson, R. (1999) 'Conclusions' in *No Frontiers: North-South Integration in Ireland*, Belfast: Democratic Dialogue, p. 89. Democratic Dialogue is a Belfast-based think-tank whose 'vision is of an

egalitarian civic society, at ease with itself and its evolving context.'
http://www.democraticdialogue.org/

14 O'Hearn, D. (2000) 'Peace Dividend, Foreign Investment, and Economic Regeneration: The Northern Irish Case', *Social Problems*, 47 (2), 184.

15 Ibid., p. 191.

16 The latest consolidated EU Directive (2004/18/EC) on public procurement was published in April 2004. See *Official Journal*, 30 April 2004, L 134/114.

17 Department of Finance and Personnel (2001) *A Review of Public Procurement, Findings and Recommendations*, Belfast: DFP.

18 The 1998 Agreement, p. 19.

19 Daly, M. and Leonard, M. (2002) *Against All Odds: Family Life on a Low Income in Ireland*, Dublin: Institute of Public Administration.

20 In this context it is interesting to note that in the immediate aftermath of the cease-fires in 1994, the Combat Poverty Agency made a submission to the Forum for Peace and Reconciliation urging a range of measures to tackle poverty in Northern Ireland on the grounds that 'poverty and social exclusion are important contributory factors which exacerbate and perpetuate violence', Combat Poverty Agency (1994) *Tackling Poverty: A Priority for Peace, Submission to the Forum for Peace and Reconciliation*, p. 3.

21 *Sharing in Progress, National Anti-Poverty Strategy* (1997) Dublin: Stationery Office, p. i.

22 UN (1995) *Report of the World Summit for Social Development (Copenhagen 6–12 March)*, New York: UN, p. 46.

23 *Sharing in Progress*, op. cit., p. 73.

24 Ibid., p. 73.

25 Ibid., p. 73.

26 Eithne Fitzgerald, Dáil Éireann, vol. 489, 21 April 1998.

27 This recommendation was particularly welcome by CORI which saw it as linking welfare rates to industrial earnings. CORI Justice Commission (2002) *NAPS Review 2002, Analysis and Critique*, Dublin: CORI.

28 Department of Finance and Personnel (1999) *Vision into Practice*, Belfast: DFP. http://www.dfpni.gov.uk/ccru/index1.htm

29 Office of the First Minister and Deputy First Minister (2002) *Interim Evaluation of New TSN: Summary and Synthesis of Report VI*, April, Belfast: Deloitte and Touche.

30 Invest Northern Ireland's new HQ is to be financed through a public-private partnership scheme and bids are expected to total £45 million. Some 500 employees will be accommodated. No consideration appears to have been given to locating this public body in a deprived area of either North or East Belfast. The assumption is that this

'modern facility that will assist us in our efforts to help strengthen Northern Ireland's economy' must be in the city centre. Chief Executive, Leslie Morrison, quoted in Business Section, *Irish News*, 16 December, 2003.

31 Office of the First Minister and Deputy First Minister (2004) *Towards an Anti-Poverty Strategy: New TSN – the Way Forward, A Consultation Document*, Belfast: Office of First Minister and Deputy First Minister, p. 11.

32 Ibid., p. 35.

33 http://www.hmso.gov.uk/acts/acts1998/80047—j.htm

34 Class discrimination is most marked in relation to educational resource allocations. A medical student at Queen's University, who is most likely to come from a middle-class family, will receive many times the unit of resource of a working-class child attending primary school on the Shankill Road. At the same time, the latter is likely to come out of school without any formal qualifications, while the former will be able to secure an income in the top decile.

35 Daly, M. (2003) NAP/incl 2003, *First Background Report on Ireland*, Belfast: School of Sociology and Social Policy, Queen's University.

36 Communication from the Commission to the Council, the European Parliament, the Economic and Social Committee and the Committee of the Regions (2001) *Report on Social Inclusion*.

37 Combat Poverty Agency (2003) *Working towards a Poverty-Free Society: Submission to the National Action Plan Against Poverty and Social Exclusion 2003–2005*, Dublin: Combat Poverty Agency, p. 5.

38 Department of the Taoiseach (2003) *National Action Plan Against Poverty and Social Exclusion 2003–2005*, Dublin: Stationery Office. p. 12.

39 *Northern Ireland Structural Funds Plan 2000–2006*, p. 8. www.europe-dfpni.gov.uk/Upload/SF_manual/sfplan2000_2006.pdf

40 Ibid., p. 89.

41 Ibid., p. 90.

42 Some co-operation exists in this field. See Central Statistics Office/Northern Ireland Statistics and Research Agency, *Ireland, North and South: A Statistical Profile*, Dublin/Belfast: Government Publications Office/NISRA.

43 The 1998 Agreement, pp. 16–18.

44 McGarry, J. and O'Leary, B. (1999) *Policing Northern Ireland: proposals for a new start*, Belfast: Blackstaff Press.

45 The 1998 Agreement, p. 22.

46 *A New Beginning in Northern Ireland: the Report of the Independent Commission on Policing in Northern Ireland*, September 1999. http://www.belfast.org.uk/report/fullreport.pdf

47   Stalker, J. (1989) *The Stalker Affair*, Harmondsworth: Penguin Books, pp. 56–57.

48   The 1998 Agreement, p. 22.

49   'Case hardening' is a widely used term in legal scholarship to describe how the impartiality and objectivity of judges may be compromised by regular exposure to similar types of cases.

50   Boyle, K., Hadden, T. and Hillyard, P. (1980) *Ten Years on in Northern Ireland: the Legal Control of Political Violence*, London: Cobden Trust, p. 62.

51   http://www.nio.gov.uk/pdf/recommendations.pdf

52   Northern Ireland Court Service (2000) Departmental Investment Strategy, Belfast: NI Court Service. http://www.nics.gov.uk/pubsec/courts/nictsdis.pdf

53   Northern Ireland Courts Service: PFI: Laganside Courts, Report by the Comptroller and Auditor General, HC 649, Session 2002–2003, 4 June 2003.

54   Northern Ireland Court Service Resource Accounts, 2002–2003. http://www.courtsni.gov.uk/

55   *Belfast Telegraph*, 15 December 2003, p. 3.

56   Hayner, Priscilla B. (2001) *Unspeakable Truths: Confronting State Terror and Atrocity*, New York, Routledge.

57   Rolston, B. (1996) *Turning the Page without Closing the Book: the Right to Truth in the Irish Context*, Dublin: Irish Reporter Publications.

58   The 1998 Agreement, p. 18.

59   Bloomfield, K. (1998) *We Will Remember Them*, Belfast: Stationery Office, p. 50.

60   Wilson, J. (1999) *A Place and a Name: Report of the Victims Commission*, Dublin: Stationery Office.

61   Rolston, B. (2002) 'Assembling the Jigsaw: Truth, Justice and Transition in the North of Ireland', *Race and Class*, 44 (1), 87–105.

62   *All Truth is Bitter: a Report of the Visit of Doctor Alex Boraine, Deputy Chairman of the South African Truth and Reconciliation Commission, to Northern Ireland* (1999), Belfast: NIACRO and Victim Support Northern Ireland.

63   *Healing Through Remembering: the Report of the Healing Through Remembering Project* (2002), Belfast.

64   Northern Ireland Human Rights Commission (2003), *Human Rights and Victims of Violence*, Belfast: Northern Ireland Human Rights Commission.

65   Eolas (2003) *Consultation Paper on Truth and Justice*, Belfast: Eolas Project.

66   'NI commission "could heal wounds"', BBC News. http://news.bbc.co.uk/1/hi/northern_ireland/3499613.stm

[67] 'Police chief calls for peace and reconciliation in Ulster', *The Guardian*, 23 February 2004.

[68] Carroll, R. (2004) 'A Telling Contribution', *The Guardian*, 9 June.

[69] South African Truth and Reconciliation Commission, *Final Report, Volume 4*, Chapter 2, 'Business and Labor', para. 161. http://bs.cyty.com/elmbs/trcbus.htm

[70] http://www.ark.ac.uk/nilt/2002/Community_Relations/MXRLGWRK.html

[71] McDonald, H. (2004) 'Blair to cut troop numbers even if political deal fails', *The Observer*, September 12.

[72] Northern Ireland Office/HM Treasury (2003) *Northern Ireland Office 2003 Departmental Report,* Cm. 5929, pp. 138–139. http://www.nio.gov.uk/pdf/deprep2003.pdf

[73] Ibid., pp. 138–139.

[74] See http://www.garda.ie/angarda/statistics/report2002/annrep2002.pdf

[75] *Hansard*, HC (Session 2002–03) vol. 415, written answers, col. 130 (4 December 2003).

[76] *Hansard*, HC (Session 1997–98), vol. 307, written answers, col. 626 (4 March 1998).

[77] *Hansard*, HC (Session 1997–98), vol. 318, written answers, col. 445 (3 November 1998).

[78] Dáil Éireann, vol. 547, 31 January 2002.

[79] Northern Ireland Affairs Committee, *The Financing of Terrorism in Northern Ireland*, Fourth Report session 2001–2002, HC 978-I.

[80] Oddly, one Sunday newspaper turned these relatively modest figures into £150 million from counterfeit goods alone. According to *The Observer*, 15 June 2003, 'Up to 100 criminal gangs are operating in Ulster and at least two-thirds are linked to the Provisional IRA, the Ulster Defence Association and other paramilitary organisations. The province has become a major UK hub for the sale and distribution of counterfeit goods, which is believed to have earned the gangs more than £150m last year.'

[81] Northern Ireland Affairs Committee, *The Financing of Terrorism in Northern Ireland*, op. cit., pp. 14–15.

[82] The Organised Crime Task Force (2003) *Assessment: Threat Assessment 2003, Serious and Organised Crime in Northern Ireland*, Belfast: NIO, p. 2.

[83] *Stevens Enquiry 3: Overview and Recommendations*, 17 April 2003; Cory, P. (2004) *Cory Collusion Inquiry Report, Patrick Finucane*, 1 April, HC 470, London: Stationary Office.

[84] On the work of Coiste na n-Iarchímí, see http://www.coiste.ie/. For reasons too complex to explore at this point, organisations working

with loyalist ex-prisoners have had less success. On this general issue, see McShane, L. (1998) *Politically motivated ex-prisoners self-help projects*, Belfast: Community Foundation for Northern Ireland; Community Foundation for Northern Ireland (2001) *A level playing field: peacebuilding through the reintegration of politically-motivated ex-prisoners*, Belfast: Community Foundation for Northern Ireland.

85   Community Foundation for Northern Ireland (2003) *Taking 'Calculated' Risks for Peace II*, Belfast: Community Foundation for Northern Ireland, pp. 47–50.

86   Violent crime, which is not politically motivated, has risen steadily in the decade since the cease-fires (see *A Commentary on the Northern Ireland Crime Statistics 2003*, Belfast: Northern Ireland Office, 2004). One element of this has been a rise in violent crimes against women (see *Gender and the Northern Ireland Criminal Justice System*, Belfast: Northern Ireland Office, 2002).

87   Quoted in McCafferty, N. (1981) *The Armagh Women*, Dublin: Co-op Books, p. 88.

88   McWilliams, M. and McKeirnan, J. (1996) *Taking Domestic Violence Seriously*, Belfast: HMSO.

89   Coulter, C. (1991) *Web of Punishment*, Dublin: Attic Press.

90   In a recent overview of the role of women in the Northern Ireland peace process, the Department of Foreign Affairs stated that the benefits of involving women in conflict resolution is 'clearly evident in Northern Ireland, where women played and continue to play a pivotal role in building peace and are essential contributors to the ongoing process of fostering reconciliation.' Anglo-Irish Division, Department of Foreign Affairs (2003), 'The role of women in the NI Peace Process', paper presented to the Council of Europe,' 1 December.

91   The obvious exception being the Women's Coalition, which had two Members elected to the first Assembly.

92   National Report of Ireland, *Special session of the United Nations General Assembly: Women 2000: Gender equality, development and peace for the 21st century*, January 2000. www.irlgov.ie/justice

93   Department of Justice, Equality and Law Reform, Draft 1, *National Plan for Women (2001–2005)*, August 2001, p. 54.

94   Keane, M. P. and McCann, M. (2001) *Exploring Differences: reflections on a model of cross-border/cross-cultural work*, Dublin: Women Educating for Transformation, p. 1.

95   National Women's Council of Ireland (2001) *Framing the Future: an integrated strategy to support women's community and voluntary organisations*, Dublin: NWCI, p. 108.

96   Northern Ireland Voluntary Trust (2001) *Where to FROM HERE: a new paradigm for the women's sector in Northern Ireland*, Belfast: NIVT, October, p. 2.

[97] Kvinna Till Kvinna (2004) *Rethink! A handbook for sustainable peace,* Stockholm, p. 15. http: www.iktk.se/publikationer/rapporter/pdf/ Rethink

[98] Keane, M. P. and McCann, M. (2001), op. cit., p. 7.

[99] Ibid., p. 24.

[100] McMinn, J. and O'Meara, L. (2000) *Research into the Sustainability of Community Women's Groups in the Six Southern Border Counties,* Dublin: Women Educating for Transformation, p. 19.

[101] Women's Support Network, 'Sustaining the Community', *Newsletter* 2 (6), May 2002, p. 2.

[102] Taillon, R. (2000) *The Social and Economic Impact of Women's Centres in Greater Belfast,* Belfast: Women's Support Network.

[103] Taillon, R. (2002) *NI Women's Organisations' Experiences of EU Funding Programmes,* Survey Report, Belfast: Women's Support Network.

[104] Taillon, R. (2000) op. cit., p. 116.

[105] Morgan, V. (2003) 'The role of women in community development in Northern Ireland', in O. Hargie and D. Dickson (eds.) *Researching the Troubles: Social Science Perspectives on the N.I. Conflict,* Edinburgh: Mainstream Publishing, p. 256.

[106] Morgan, V. (2002) 'Women and a "New" Northern Ireland', in J. Neuheiser and S. Wolff (eds.), *Peace At Last? The Impact of the Good Friday Agreement on Northern Ireland,* New York and Oxford: Berghahn Books, p. 165.

[107] Smyth, M. (1998) *Half the Battle: Understanding the Impact of the Troubles on Children and Young People,* Derry: INCORE. http://cain.ulst.ac.uk/issues/violence/cts/smyth.htm

[108] Curtis, L. (1982) *They Shoot Children: The Use of Rubber and Plastic Bullets in the North of Ireland,* London: Information on Ireland.

[109] Smyth, M. and Scott, M. (2001) *The YouthQuest 2000 Survey: A report on young people's views and experiences in Northern Ireland,* Belfast: Community Conflict Impact on Children/Joint Society for a Common Cause.

[110] Memorandum submitted by the Northern Ireland Anti Poverty Network (CP 15), Select Committee on Work and Pensions, Written Evidence. http://www.parliament.the-stationery-office.co.uk/pa/cm200304/cmselect/cmworpen/85/85we24.htm

[111] Kelly, P. (2000) 'Whose Peace is it anyway? Children's Rights in the New Political Dispensation', *childRIGHT*, 163, 15–17. http://www.childrenslawcentre.org/ArticleforChildright.htm

[112] *Protecting Children and Young People's Rights in the Bill of Rights for Northern Ireland: a Briefing Paper for the Children and Young People's*

Sector (2003) Belfast: Children and Young People's Sector Bill of Rights Group.
http://www.childrenslawcentre.org/BillofRightsAdultVersion.htm

113 *Review of the Criminal Justice System in Northern Ireland* (2000), Belfast: HMSO, para. 9.53, p. 203.
http://www.nio.gov.uk/pdf/mainreport.pdf

114 See statement of PSNI Community Safety Branch.
http://www.psni.police.uk/index/about_psni/pg_community_involveme nt_branch.htm

115 Community Foundation for Northern Ireland (2003), op. cit., p. 74.

116 Ibid., p. 15. That Peace II has continued to fail to meet the needs in unionist areas is accepted by Shaun Henry of the Secretariat of the Special EU Programmes Body in Belfast. See 'Protestants missing out on peace funding', *Belfast Telegraph*, 14 September 2004.

117 Ibid., p. 27.

118 Ibid., p. 12.

119 Ibid., p. 76.

120 Harvey, B. (2003) *Review of the Peace II Programme*, York: Joseph Rowntree Charitable Trust, p. 55.

121 Quoted in Rolston, B. (1990) 'Political Vetting: an Overview', in Political Vetting of Community Work Group, *The Political Vetting of Community Work in Northern Ireland*, Belfast: Northern Ireland Council for Voluntary Action, p. 3.

122 *First Report of the Independent Monitoring Commission* (2004), London: The Stationery Office, p. 40.

123 Harvey, B. (2003), op. cit., p. 33.

124 Ibid., p. 56.

125 Belloni, R. (2001) 'Civil Society and Peacebuilding in Bosnia and Herzogovina', *Journal of Peace Research*, 38 (2), pp. 163–180.

126 Moore, D. (2000) 'Levelling the Playing Fields and Embedding Illusions: "Post-Conflict" Discourse and Neo-liberal "Development" in War-torn Africa', *Review of African Political Economy*, 83, pp. 11–28.

127 Stiefel, M. (1999) *Rebuilding after war: Lessons from WSP*, Geneva: War-torn Societies Project.
http://wsp.dataweb.ch/wsp_publication/toc-6.htm

128 Connor, W. (1993) *Ethnonationalism: The Quest for Understanding*, Princeton: Princeton University Press. See also Conversi, D. (ed.) (2004) *Ethnonationalism in the Contemporary World: Walker Connor and the Study of Nationalism*, London: Routledge.

Chapter 7

Transcending Poverty and Conflict

This review of the international research evidence on poverty and conflict points to several major conclusions. The relationship between poverty and conflict is two-way and not necessarily simultaneous. At times poverty can be seen to be the dominant causative factor that precipitates violent conflict when disadvantaged minorities (and sometimes majorities) express their grievances and receive a negative response. On the other hand, conflicts such as civil wars – now the dominant form of military conflict globally – produce and extend poverty.

Poverty on its own is an insufficient predictor of conflict, and the wealthier the society, the less likely that poverty is a trigger for conflict, especially armed conflict. With developed welfare states and centralised policing, Ireland, North and South, should not be conflict prone. But the international evidence tells us that when poverty is combined with ethnic, religious or unresolved national divisions, armed conflicts are much more likely. Strong states may act to both limit conflict and to perpetuate it in particular forms. Special geographical and regional factors, often associated with border areas or 'conflict commodities', may provide additional resources and incentives for armed conflict.

Inequality is also implicated in generating conflict by increasing social instability and disorder. The extent of inequality and increases in inequality both contribute to the growth of violence, including domestic violence, and other types of crime. This association has been observed for rich countries as well as developing countries.

One of the most important lessons from the poverty and conflict literature reviewed in this report is that peace agreements are unstable and very often end with another round of conflict. Although such failures are usually understood as *political* breakdowns, it is clear from our review of reconstruction that a whole range of factors can be involved. Reconstruction tends to prioritise the repair of damaged infrastructure and the re-establishment of economic activity using models required by international financial institutions. Economic development aid is highly conditional and there is increasing consensus that those conditions need to embrace conflict resolution and prevention.

In addition to stable democratic political arrangements, peace-building involves poverty reduction, law and criminal justice reform, respect for human rights, and participatory forms of governance that actively respond to the legacies of past conflicts and continuing social divisions and sources of friction. The international agencies, including the UN, have paid increasing attention to the role of women in social and economic reconstruction, and in political institutions. Economic development and political arrangements that simply *reproduce* divisions will not build peace or prevent conflicts from re-emerging in the future.

In Chapter 4 we presented an assessment of the changing context of poverty, inequality and the conflict in Ireland, as well as discussing the limited evidence on the legacies of the conflict. Clearly there is scope for more targeted research into some of the questions raised and areas covered. In particular, as Chapter 5 shows, systematic evidence on how the experience of conflict relates to poverty has only recently become available. Significantly, increased risks of poverty are associated with forced house moves and being intimidated out of the workplace. They are especially associated with multiple experience of death and injury of people close to the victim and with the witnessing of a killing.

As discussed in Chapter 6, major challenges remain for the transcending of poverty and conflict in Ireland. These challenges cut across all sectors of society. The peace process has yet to establish stable political institutions. Major issues relating to the conflict and its management remain. There is continuing argument over the reform of policing and criminal justice. Progress on the development of a human rights culture has been limited. And there is uncertainty on the possible role of a truth commission in dealing with the past. Furthermore, Northern Ireland remains a highly militarised society.

In terms of social rights and economic reconstruction, very little has changed for people living in the most economically marginalised areas, particularly the border region. To some extent, the lack of an economic 'peace dividend' for those communities is offset by the sense that they are moving forward in terms of political representation and gains. But electoral advances as such are no substitute for working alongside political opponents within an agreed institutional framework, or for the exercise of power and responsibility that come with government. This is especially the case for nationalist areas. In contrast, loyalist communities most affected by the conflict have seen neither an economic peace dividend nor an on-going and developing political dividend.

Overall, this is a potentially unstable situation that needs sustained, long-term intervention at local level. The primary challenge is to tackle poverty and social exclusion in the communities most affected by decades of armed conflict. This means 'mainstreaming' peace-building and conflict resolution within anti-poverty strategies and those international programmes ostensibly concerned with reconstruction. Some are opposed to this aim because they see it as, in effect, 'rewarding terrorism'. The evidence, however, is that if poverty and continuing conflict are not addressed, they may act as incubators of further cycles of violent actions, whether disordered, reactive or part of an organised movement.

Ireland, North and South, therefore needs anti-poverty policies that incorporate conflict resolution and conflict prevention. Below we suggest a basic framework of what needs to be addressed.

Reconstruction

We recommend that successful peace-building should involve the following:

- Reconstruction as a theme in programmes of government, North and South.

- Recognition that peace-building requires sustained commitment, long-term planning, and mainstream funding.

- Grass-roots participation based on community development principles as a *sine qua non* of reconstruction.

- Support for civil society organisations throughout Ireland in constructing programmes of action designed to foster reconciliation, build on existing positive social relationships and prevent violent conflict.

Poverty and inequality

As potential incubators of conflict, poverty and inequality should be tackled through:

- Long-term objectives for reducing levels of poverty and inequality through progressive taxation policies, increased levels of universal benefits and redistribution of both public and private resources.

- Identification of poverty reduction targets for specific groups whose poverty is conflict-related, including both the victims and perpetrators of violence.

- Incorporation of conflict reduction performance indicators in anti-poverty programmes.

- The inclusion of a North-South common chapter in reports to the EU on progress on poverty reduction and social inclusion.

Women, children and young people

Particular emphasis should be placed on:

- Prioritisation of an increased role for women in all forms of reconstruction through policies to increase women's political and civic representation, and universal child-care provision.

- Gender mainstreaming of all policies.

- Recognition of the specific effects of the conflict on women, children and young people and support measures dedicated to their full integration.

Sectarianism

In order to prevent the continuing reproduction of sectarianism, we recommend:

- Instigation of a robust anti-sectarian agenda at all levels, including in the heart of government and the civil service.

- Rigorous monitoring of sectarian attacks, intimidation and violence.

- Establishment of secular schooling outside church control that will support parents, students and teachers committed to anti-sectarian schooling.

Economic development

In order that economic development benefits the communities most affected by the conflict, policies should focus on the following:

- Incentives to bring jobs to the border region and other areas of economic marginalisation.

- Use of public procurement to achieve the objectives of peace-building, including business development and employment in marginalised areas.

- Recognition that participation rates need to increase but that there are limits to this which are directly related to the conflict.

- Increasing opportunities for the social inclusion of groups most affected by conflict through expansion of the social economy.

- Involvement of all social partners, especially the business community, in developing active partnerships with areas most affected by conflict.

- The development of infrastructure and core communications and distributional services which benefit all the people who share the island of Ireland.

- Production, on a routine basis, of comparative North/South social and economic statistics that can inform policy making in relation to socially and economically marginalised groups and areas. The border region is a priority in this respect.

Marginalised groups

In relation to specific groups marginalised by the conflict we recommend:

- Stimulation of exchanges between socially and economically marginalised communities on a North/South basis, and between Ireland and other parts of the world engaged in conflict resolution.

- Recognition of the physical and mental health issues arising from poverty and conflict, including the specific problem of suicide among younger people.

- Development of collaborative research and information on social needs with groups and communities most affected by the conflict.

Human rights and security

We recommend that the following should be emphasised:

- Promotion of a human rights culture, including social and economic rights, through robust support of human rights commissions, North and South, and efforts to come to terms with past human rights abuses.

- Reduction of public expenditure on law enforcement agencies and increase in spending on social and economic security.

- Expansion of labour market opportunities for politically motivated ex-prisoners.